The Beekeeping Bible

[5 in 1]

The Ultimate Collection to Learn How to Start Your First Bee Colony to Produce Honey in Abundance | Includes +100 Beeswax and Propolis Projects

Garth Burke

Table of Contents

Book 1

The Beekeeping for Beginners

Introduction

The technique of maintaining bee colonies to accomplish preferred goals is known as beekeeping, sometimes known as apiculture. The most prevalent species of domesticated bee is the honeybee. Additionally, stingless bees and other honey-producing bees are saved. Apiculture is permitted anywhere; bees can be kept in towns, farms, ranches, rangelands, deserts, or even woods. Amazingly, city beekeepers may even place their hives on roofs in heavily populated cities!

The bees shouldn't be held, so why do it? Within the agricultural and natural ecosystems, bees are crucial. In addition to producing valuable and healthy products, bees and other pollinators like butterflies contribute to the pollination of about 75% of the plants that provide 90% of the world's food. A beekeeper or apiarist is the person who maintains the beehives.

Chapter 1
Introduction to Beekeeping

Since the beginning of time, people have consumed honey. It is first obtained from swarms of wild honeybees. As a result, this is known as honey harvesting or hunting. The entire bee colony must be destroyed in order to accumulate honey. The natural hives had been broken into, and the bees were suppressed using smoke. Later, people learned that instead of searching for bees in the wild, they could build a hive or residence nearby. Beginning with pottery jars, woven straw baskets, wood bins, and hole logs, they first preserved bees in these materials.

The honey, larvae, eggs, and other components that were contained in the honeycombs were all hammered out during the harvesting process. After that, a sieve was used to filter the liquid honey. Because every colony was destroyed along with the queen at harvest, there was no continuity of production. People began to understand bee colonies and biology in the 18th century, which made the creation of mobile hives more appealing. These hives made it possible to collect honey without endangering the colony.

The development of a mobile comb hive by Lorenzo Langstroth throughout the nineteenth century led to a breakthrough in beekeeping. In a rectangular hive box, he created a set of timber frames that allowed a beekeeper to gently remove the honeycombs and retrieve the honey without damaging the combs. After harvesting, the empty combs were put back in the hives for the bees to top off once more. Additionally, people had the ability to divide a colony rather of relying solely on spontaneous swarming.

Business beekeeping was made possible by the invention of the mobile comb hive and the creation of the wax-comb foundation, including the beginning comb that bees build on and the use of centrifuges for extracting honey, among other things. The increase in honey production and colony efficiency can be attributed to the prevalence, prevention, and control of bee diseases, the use of artificial insemination of queens and pollen substitutes to maintain healthy colonies. The nineteenth century saw the beginning of commercial beekeeping. Industrial apiarists possess a lot of hives—possibly hundreds of them—that yield a lot of honey.

Types of Beekeeping

Natural Beekeeping

Herbal beekeeping is centered around mimicking the bees' natural habitat. Instead of forcing them into an artificial environment, a herbal beekeeper uses techniques and strategies that align with how bees live in the wild. This includes minimizing disturbances to the hive and allowing the colony to survive winter on their own honey rather than artificial food. Natural materials are preferred for the comb, and chemical treatments are avoided as much as possible. Essential oils may be used to combat mites and diseases instead.

Backyard or Urban Beekeeping

Backyard beekeeping refers to maintaining bee colonies in an urban environment. It is ambitioto acquire honey and different bee merchandise by utilizing small-scale colonies. City beekeeping is on the rise in many elements of the sector.

Indoor Beekeeping

The practice of housing honey bee hives indoors has become increasingly popular. Whether it is due to limited space, the need for constant observation, or the slow season for beekeeping, many beekeepers are now utilizing advanced in-house hives designed specifically for the thriving of their colonies. In colder months, some commercial beekeepers even relocate their hives to specialized warehouses with controlled levels of moisture, light, and temperature to ensure the health of their colonies. These measures serve as crucial support for sustaining strong and productive bee populations throughout the year.

Legal Obligations of Beekeepers

Beekeeping is a growing hobby, with many people becoming beekeepers in their backyards. Bees are an important part of our ecosystem, and their pollination is vital for our food supply. But keeping bees can come with some legal obligations that beekeepers must be aware of. In addition, there are important steps you should take to protect yourself from lawsuits if your bees become a nuisance to your neighbors.

You can't be a beekeeper without registering. Everyone needs to register as a beekeeper, even if they just keep their bees in their backyard. Registration is compulsory and free, so you don't have an excuse for not doing it.

Registering your apiary is important for several reasons:

- It helps ensure the safety of people around the colony, including yourself and others that might visit your apiary.

- Knowing how many colonies you have will help authorities determine whether they need to issue special warnings or take other measures around your area if something goes wrong with your colony, and it must be destroyed or relocated.

You must register your bees with the authorities. This may be a local council, state, or federal agency, or it could be a combination of these if you live in an urban area. For example, beekeepers in Brisbane will need to register their hives with Brisbane City Council. Even further north on the Gold Coast there are separate registration requirements for the Queensland Environmental Protection Agency (EPA).

Registration is free and usually takes about five minutes to complete online. If you don't do this, it's illegal! In some states and territories, you can also get financial assistance from government agencies if you lose all your bees due to unforeseen circumstances such as disease outbreaks or heavy rains destroying your apiary (bee yard).

The registration includes the location of the bees and the identity of the owner. If a beekeeper wants to move his or her hive, he or she must notify us within two days before doing so and provide a description of how it's been moved, including from where to where and by what means.

In addition to these legal obligations, beekeepers should also be aware that:

- The number of bees allowed in each hive depends on location as well as time of year.

Registration is important to track the spread of diseases among honeybees. Bees can be very mobile, so it is necessary to know who owns them, where they are located, and what diseases they might have. By registering your bees, you will help prevent the spread of bee diseases and increase safety for your own bees.

All beekeepers should take their registration duty seriously and comply on time. Registration is important for many reasons, including the following:

- The registration of your hives allows you to track the spread of the disease. This information can help beekeepers and government officials decide how best to address bees in their area, as well as allow people who have had contact with diseased bees to know if they need medical attention.

- Beekeepers who are registered receive subsidies from their local governments that allow them to buy tools or equipment necessary for beekeeping, such as honey extractors or queen bees. Some states or countries may offer these subsidies only after a certain number of years spent maintaining an apiary (or beehive).

- It's also possible that some governments may offer training courses specifically designed for new beekeepers who have not yet completed five years' worth of experience in this field; these courses might teach them how best to manage pests without harming other insects like butterflies or moths at their local farmlands where crops grow naturally without pesticides sprayed onto them daily during daylight hours throughout springtime months only when sunshine reaches at least 80% full strength every hour throughout daytimes which happen every single day between March 21st through October 31st each year so that all plants grow properly before winter arrives again next year around June 1st - September 30th depending upon whether there's enough rain during these periods; otherwise they'll die out completely until next year when we start over again!

Beekeeping is a great way to make extra money, but it can be dangerous if you don't follow the rules. If you are thinking about starting a beekeeping business or hobby, you should know about your legal obligations as a beekeeper.

Chapter 2
Learning About Bees

For a farm herd, American gold honey (Apis mellifera ligustica) is perhaps the best investment. Large honey producers who tolerate winter well in frigid areas, feed gently, have strong tolerance to illness and natural enemies. In contrast to other types, they seem to be less susceptible to the connection.

Today, the majority of packaged beehives exclusively sell tested queens in packages of two and three pounds. In 1974, such a kit, appropriately referred to as "nuc," was available for between $ 10 and $ 12. The businesses operating in this booming industry are situated in regions with hot weather all year round, and they transport bees between April 1 and June 1 (before this time, the weather is too cold, and the summer bees are carried after), when they would otherwise be roasted.

You will need to prepare your hair before purchasing your bees (wrap the packages together, which I'm sure your post office likes). To put it another way, start putting your beekeeping supplies together once you've ordered your first colony.

Better Know A Bee

Honey bees consist of three different species of bees.:

- Worker
- Drone
- Queen

Each member of the bee colony plays a significant part and carries out a specialized function.

Queen Bee

It can be identified by its abdomen, which is often smooth, lengthy, and far beyond its folded wings.

Role Of the Queen Bee

The Queen Bee plays a crucial role in the hive's functioning. As the only breeding female, she is responsible for producing eggs starting from early spring when workers bring home new pollen. She can lay up to 2,000 eggs per day at her most productive. Although queens can live up to five years, they typically only last two to three years before being replaced due to decreased fertility. To avoid an overabundance of drones, beekeepers often replace older queens every year or two. While experienced beekeepers may be able to produce their own high-quality queens, it is recommended for beginners to purchase queens from reputable suppliers.

What is a Queen Substance?

A pheromone known as a queen substance is also produced by queen bees. As food is shared among the bees in the hives, this chemical mixture is transferred from bee to bee one by one. Due to a drop in pheromone levels, workers will become aware of the absence of the queen bee if it is taken from the colony within a few hours.

When a queen is absent, the need to produce a new "emergency" queen from the tiniest larvae available arises quickly (1-3 days). Additionally, this pheromone prevents workers' ovaries from developing normally. Some people might be lay employees now that the queen is gone. The quantity of pheromones the queen produces is also rated by the workers. Workers may see it as being of inferior quality and start making plans to replace it if they only receive an insufficient dose each day. To make it simple to locate and verify whether it has been replaced, beekeepers frequently color the queen's breast.

What Are Worker Bees?

The majority of bees in a beehive are workers. These female bees are unable to reproduce and make up the largest population in the hive. While they cannot lay eggs, they play important roles in the colony by performing a variety of tasks:

- They collect all the pollen and nectar that was transported into the hive, turning the nectar into honey.

- Create royal jelly to feed the larvae and the queen.

- Additionally, they are susceptible to the demands of larvae and queens.

- Mature larval cells are only used for pupation, and the hive is cleaned out of dirt and dead bees.

- Worker bees protect the hives from intruders and maintain ideal conditions by heating, cooling, and ventilating them.

On the sides of their heads, the workers have three basic eyes (ocelli) alongside well-developed complex eyes. To sip nectar from flowers, they have long, well-developed tongues.

Worker Bee Lifespan

Typically, spring and early summer workers have a lifespan of five to six weeks. They labor in the hive for the first two weeks of their existence as domestic bees.

The rest of the time they are out in the wild, searching for food. Workers who become mature in the late fall can survive well the following spring. During the winter, the bee queen should be kept warm by a body group. They will be responsible for raising the first generation of baby bees the next year once laying has resumed.

What Are Drones?

Drones are male bees. The only task of the drone is to fertilize a small sheep.

- clearly stronger and larger than the workers.

- They differ from workers and queens in that they have a little longer antenna and huge, distinctive eyes that connect at the top of their heads.

- Usually, their mouth parts recede.

- Drone cells are clearly larger than worker cells when they arise from unfertilized eggs.

- Drones don't create wax, tend to have pups, or gather pollen or nectar. They consume the honeycombs of the hive directly or ask the worker bees for sustenance.

- They are primarily bred in the spring and summer, about four weeks before the new queens emerge, to make sure that there are plenty of drones available for the developing queens.

- They normally divide their day into feeding and rest times, as well as the protection of breeding grounds known as drone assembly zones.

As summer comes to a close and the food supply dwindles, the production of drones will cease. Typically, drones are supported and protected by worker bees within the hive before winter arrives. However, if the queen is lost, the colony may produce eggs that result in only male drones. This can be detrimental to the colony's survival. In a last-ditch effort to continue their genetic line, the colony may create many drones in hopes of mating with a virgin queen from another colony.

Chapter 3
Becoming A Beekeeper

The Benefits of Beekeeping

Honey and Other Bee Products

When we hear about beekeeping, honey is usually the first thing that comes to mind. It is the most well-known product from bee colonies and is known for its high levels of antioxidants and other beneficial nutrients. However, there are other valuable products that come from bees, such as wax, pollen, and propolis. These can be used to make various products like candles, soaps, lip balms, and hair care items. In today's market, all bee products have a high value. With modern equipment, beekeeping has become more advanced and accessible for potential buyers

Crops Pollination

Plants expect fertilization to imitate. Bumblebees are the most significant pollinators on the planet. Various harvests like blueberries, almonds, avocadoes, apples, and cherries rely altogether upon them. They fertilize crops normally as they search for nectar and dust. Research shows that honey bees contribute around $20 to US crop creation.

Source of Income

Is keeping bees a good idea? Absolutely! It can be a highly beneficial pursuit, depending on the number of hives and amount of honey produced. Some professional beekeepers also earn income by renting out their hives for pollination services to farmers, while others sell bees to other beekeepers.

An Inexpensive Venture

Despite the underlying beginning up cost, apiculture requires low upkeep. Bumblebees are super specialists regarding running the hive and making honey. They just require beneficial taking care of in the midst of shortage.

Bees need us

Similarly, as we want the honey bees for fertilization and their items, they likewise need us to shield them from bothers, pesticides, poisons, and different dangers. They require safe water sources and safe blossoming plants to search. A decent beekeeper helps the honey bees by really focusing on their hives and guaranteeing the general climate is protected.

- the benefits of having a winger
- the possible disadvantages of being a beekeeper

Chapter 4
The Year of The Beekeeper

In most areas, seasonal honey bees can be found, and therefore the beekeeper's responsibilities are based on the calendar. While it is important to organize your beekeeping tasks according to the season, keep in mind that the seasons may vary by location. "Spring" in North Dakota doesn't start until after March 21/22, and Florida's "summer" lasts longer than Alaska's brief ten-week season. Throughout the year, it's crucial to monitor your bees closely. The construction and normal daily activity of their hive should be disrupted as little as possible.

Spring Tasks

- Beekeeping can begin in early spring, when bees are more abundant. Make plans for your hive, buy or build it, and join local beekeeping societies in late winter.

- As long as the bees are getting enough food, don't stop. You must feed food for them until flowering flowers are present to offer nectar, as they will have depleted their honey stores over the winter.

- Keep a few empty hives on hand in case the bees decide to swarm and need a new home. It's possible to lose bees if you don't follow these instructions. Bees swarm and migrate in the spring.

- If a hive is already established, honey can be harvested from the comb when the flowers are blossoming.

- Check your hive for a stable brood pattern and replace your queen if you fear she has died. •

- Aim to equalize the number of bees in each of your hives, if you have more than one.

Summer Tasks

- Your bees will take care of themselves during the summer, but you'll need to check up on them every few weeks to make sure they're healthy and avoid major concerns.

- The bees will be continuously on the lookout for nectar, so you should stop feeding them now.

- Make regular checks to ensure that your hives have access to water.

- Be on the lookout for hives that are stronger than others stealing weaker ones.

- Make periodic checks to ensure that the queen is producing enough eggs.

- Keep an eye out for Varroa mites.

- When using foundationless or top bar procedures, make sure your combs are hanging straight.

- Honey harvest.

Autumn Tasks

- During this time of year, honey harvesting is at its peak and bees are preparing for winter.

- Make sure the bees have enough food for the winter by harvesting honey.

- Look at the combs to see if there are any interesting brood patterns.

- Keep an eye out for sickness; cure or discard combs that are infected.

- As long as the bees are disease-free, they can be added to stronger colonies.

- Make sure that the hive's entrance is smaller and that mouse guards are in place. Take care of any pest and disease control measures that may be necessary.

- After flowering plants and nectar have run out, begin feeding the bees.

- Keep the hive from being blown around by the wind during the winter months but allow for proper ventilation.

- Make sure the hives aren't blown over by winter winds by putting weights on their tops.

Winter Tasks

- You'll help your bee colony settle in and warm up for the long, cold winter ahead before it's too late.

- All disease treatments must be completed before a patient can be discharged.

- It's important to protect the hives from the wind.

- Check your hives often for wind damage and make sure there is adequate ventilation as winter approaches. Your bees can handle the cold, but if you completely shut the hives, condensation will set in and decimate the bee population.

- Keep an eye on the bees in warmer weather to make sure they have enough honey for sustenance. Put in pollen patties or some other sort of food when they're low on nectar.

- Purchase new beekeeping supplies and equipment. Late February or early March is typically the best time to place these orders in order to have them delivered in time for spring.

Chapter 5
FAQ

Beekeeping is becoming an increasingly popular pastime. Some questions on the subject reoccur - these are a few that deserve to be addressed before taking your initial steps in this field.

1.) What are the fundamentals?

The first thing that anyone considering entering this sector asks is, "What is beekeeping?" It is an agricultural operation that entails rearing bees to gather honey.

2.) Is this a difficult job to perform?

This is a hobby that requires initial motivation. Some people are fascinated by bees from the outset, while others become more interested as they learn about them. It's often followed by training in schools and with professionals. Or by reading a book such as this one. We also cannot ignore the project's financial implications. Indeed, you must budget for and purchase the appropriate equipment (overalls, jars to store honey, gloves, a beehive, a honey extractor, etc.).

3.) How long do bees live?

A colony consists of between 30,000 and 80,000 bees. The queen can live up to five years, while the workers live just thirty-five days in the spring and summer, and four months in the fall and winter. Males who are only present in the colony during the spring and summer would live for four or five months.

4.) How does a bee produce honey?

The work in the hive is evenly distributed: worker bees collect nectar and transport it to the hive, other workers distribute the nectar within the hive, and salivation transforms the honey nectar.

5.) How many species of bee are there?

There are almost 20,000 species worldwide, although not all are "exploited." Just a handful are bred, including Apis mellifera mellifera, black bees, Apis mellifera Carnica, and Apis mellifera Caucasica.

6.) When a jar of honey is labeled "organic", was the honey foraged in an organic environment?

No, not necessarily, because organic honey is defined as honey produced by bees that have not been treated with antibiotics.

7.) What diseases do bees suffer from?

As beekeeping becomes a passion, one must also become well-versed in the intricacies of bees and their vulnerabilities. The fear of many novice beekeepers is the prevalence of bee diseases. These infections can decimate an entire colony if not addressed promptly. In Chapter Six, we will delve into the details of various bee diseases and provide preventative measures to maintain a healthy apiary. Having knowledge on hive maintenance and bee treatment is crucial in preventing or handling such situations

8.) Why does honey come in many colors, scents, flavors, and how are they different?

Real honey collected from wild bees, or domesticated honey bees, has no difference in composition and the nutritional values are similar, but the properties, color, smell, taste, and crystallization differ according to the type of flower the bees collected their nectar from.

- Honey from longan flowers is honey that smells sweet. It's the most popular, and it can be stored for a long time. It does not change color and does not crystallize.

- Honey from wildflowers is fragrant honey. When new, it is usually light yellow. It gradually turns darker over time. If stored for a long time, it may crystallize.

- Honey from sunflowers is honey that has a distinctive aroma and a pale-yellow color. It is the easiest to crystallize. It's allowed to crystallize to be used as honey cream or honey jam. This type of honey is favored by some people as it can be used as a spread in bread.

- Honey from sesame flowers is honey that smells like honey from longan flowers. You can leave it for a long time to crystallize.

9.) What can I do with a jar of honey that has crystallized?

Crystallized honey has not lost its nutritional qualities or flavor. To restore its creaminess, simply place the jar in hot water until it becomes completely liquid again. Or, as noted in number (8) above, you can use it as a spread on your pastries.

10.) What is the difference between wild honey and farmed honey?

It's no different because, in both cases, the bees are allowed to collect nectar naturally. Wild honey cannot be distinguished from farmed honey. Besides, nowadays it's very hard to find wild honey because the forests are steadily decreasing.

However, as a specialty apiary, you can set up an orchard (a longan garden in March or a sunflower field during the month of October, etc.). Honey bees naturally go to places where they can find the most nectar.

11.) What can honey be used for?

It can be used as a substitute for sugar in tea, coffee, Ovaltine, or in beverages such as honey and lemon. It can be used for cooking, such as marinating meat, pork, or making salad dressings. It is used to make desserts such as toast topping, pancakes, etc.

Additionally, it is used to make cosmetics such as hair treatments and face paint. It is also highly prized in the herbal industry as it is an essential component in making some vegetable smoothies, juices, etc.

Or simply eat it raw. Eating honey helps nourish the body.

12.) What is bee pollen?

Bee pollen is pollen that is attached to the legs of bees. Beekeepers harvest pollen from bees by the use of an extra-large comb that is kept in the doorway of their hives. When bees fly past it, the pollen is knocked off their legs and collected in a collection bucket below. This is then sold to be processed and sold as a dietary supplement.

13.) Who should choose bee pollen?

- People who have frequent colds.

- People who want to maintain healthy nails, hair, and skin.

- People who work hard, who have to use their brain for a long time or are exposed to stress.

- Children who do not like to eat vegetables.

- Adults who want to avoid meat, milk, eggs.

14.) Does bee pollen have any health benefits?

Bee pollen has the following health benefits:

- Helps the body to be strong, refreshed, and rejuvenated.

- Helps treat allergies, high blood pressure.

- Nourishes the hair and the skin.

Note: Because it is a dietary supplement, it should be eaten continuously to see results.

15.) What is royal jelly?

Royal jelly is a food that the worker bees produce for the queen bee. This is the queen bee's food. It is a creamy white liquid. In royal jelly, there are many nutrients such as carbohydrates, proteins, and many vitamins.

16.) What are the benefits of royal jelly?

Royal jelly has the following benefits:

- Nourishes the brain.

- Strengthens the body.

- Helps you feel refreshed.

- Relieves fatigue.

17.) What are the differences between bees and wasps?

You are enjoying your land in the summer when suddenly, a small hum is detected. and you discover a "honeycomb" nest by the pool, in a tree, or beneath your porch. It's entirely possible that it belongs to wasps rather than bees. Bees and wasps are commonly misunderstood. These insects can certainly appear to be the same at first glance. Here are various methods to identify them:

Bees

A bee's body is short, hairy, and has black bands lining its abdomen. The color of the gap between its stripes might vary according on the species, from dark brown to yellow. It is about 12 mm in size.

A swarm, which consists of several thousand bees, is a collection of bees that have left a hive. Bees create a honey-filled hive. Bees aren't drawn to our food and hardly ever sting. A bee dies after stinging, and her stinger has a hook that stays in the victim's skin.

Wasps

These insects don't have as much hair as bees. They are bright yellow in color with sharp black lines and an abdomen that is obviously separate from the thorax (hence the expression "having a wasp waist"). They come in sizes ranging from 10 to 25 mm.

By biting onto wood fibers and creating a paste with their saliva, wasps build their nests out of paper pulp. Wasp nests may be exposed, underground, or buried inside a wall. Wasps are more aggressive than bees, and they are drawn to our food. They may sting repeatedly and do so without any hesitation.

Do you know where a wasp or bee nest is? Avoid approaching it and causing it any disturbance; instead, keep an eye out to see what's happening there.

Early in the spring, the young queen departs from her hiding place and sets out to find a suitable location for her colony. When she locates the location, she starts to construct the nest and deposit eggs. The nest can currently be readily removed because it is little.

As the workers exit from the nest to search nourishment for the new larvae, the population grows during the summer, which also affects the comings and goings. It is considerably more difficult and dangerous to remove the nest.

Relax if you come into a wasp or bee nest in the fall; all save the young queens, who will carry on the species, are at the conclusion of their life cycles during this time. They will undoubtedly depart soon to seek shelter in a winter shelter, though.

Warning! There are always risks involved with removing a nest by hand or preventing the insects from entering. Just be careful. Better still, get specialists to handle the pest control instead.

18.) How can you prevent yourself from being stung by bees?

Prevention

These insects sting for self-defense. If a bee bothers you, avoid any sudden movement. If it lands on you, let it go on its own or gently push it away. If you've disturbed a nest, get away as quickly as possible.

In nature

Sugary meals should be kept in tightly closed containers since adult bees need sugar/nectar to sustain themselves and to carry pollen to the colony's larvae. Keep your garments free of strong odors. Watch what you eat carefully, especially what kids eat. Make sure there are no bees present before consuming any juice or sweet alcoholic beverage. The sting of a bee might penetrate your mouth or throat.

opt for long clothing. Tie your hair up. If required, wear a cap with a mosquito net. Some nests are near to the ground, so don't go barefoot. Open the windows if a bee flies inside the vehicle. It'll emerge on its own.

In the house

- Use trash containers with lids.
- No table garbage should be left lying around.
- Make sure your home's windows are fully covered with screens.

As an apiarist

This has been discussed in detail in Chapter Three. A smoker is an important tool for an apiarist and will allow you to do your job without the bees bothering you too much.

19.) What should be done in the event of a bee sting?

Check the sting site. Around the sting site, most people experience redness, pain, and edema. This reaction is typical, and despite the fact that it could be extremely unsettling, it will pass within a few hours or days.

Take painkillers and only use cold compresses (acetaminophen). However, seek medical advice if the local responses are severe or are accompanied by fever or an infection in the area.

20.) Should I worry if I get stung?

Occasionally, after getting stung by a bee, you should be concerned. When this happens, the reaction shifts away from the sting site and becomes unusual and concerning. Swelling of the face, widespread skin redness, changes in voice, trouble breathing or swallowing, weakness, continuous vomiting, loss of consciousness, or shock are all indications of a significant reaction. A potentially fatal reaction like this might happen just a few minutes after the bite. If any of these symptoms are present, take immediate action by administering an EpiPen® (which is available at pharmacies without a prescription), consuming Benadryl®, and visiting the closest emergency room. Make an ambulance call if necessary.

People who are allergic to bee stings frequently experience these symptoms. If stung by the same type of bee again, someone who has previously experienced an allergic reaction is at a high risk of experiencing one that is severe or similar. Have you ever seen a sign or indicators of allergies after being bitten by an insect? If you have any such worries, consult your physician.

Consult an allergist if you've ever had a bad response to a bee sting or an insect bite.

Remember, nevertheless, that these reactions are uncommon. The great majority of bee stung victims only endure little pain and discomfort, which is typically manageable.

conclusion

Beekeeping not only helps in pollination, but you can harvest the honey for your own personal use or commercial use. It is quite an exciting backyard activity. However, it can be a bit intimidating at first. Don't worry about getting stung; once you get used to having them around, it will feel so much easier. And the more you learn about the bees and study them, the better you'll become in keeping bees and harvesting honey.

Book 2

Beehive Alchemy

Introduction

Beehive Alchemy is the term used to describe the process by which bees use their combined efforts to perform tasks that are difficult or impossible for the individual bees. This is largely due to the advantages of their teamwork over individual effort, such as increased safety, decreased risk of failure and increased efficiency. Bees have also been known to perform tasks to improve other aspects of their lives.

In recent years, scientists have begun studying whether bees can effectively learn from each other and be inspired by what they see in others. They have also begun studying the instructions that bees follow when performing various tasks, with the hopes of finding out how they carry-out these tasks. The idea has also been suggested that some of these actions may be beneficial to man due to their high usefulness. The idea of bees carrying-out an action individually or via teamwork has been around since the concept of alchemy was first envisioned. In fact, it is believed that some of the first alchemists might have been inspired by the everyday tasks of bees and their ability to perform their tasks in such a way that is nothing short of miraculous. Most would agree that the art of alchemy comes from practical experience and a higher power.

How did it start?

Beehive Alchemy started in early 2009. After a week of beekeeping, I had accumulated a large amount of knowledge regarding beekeeping, but I wanted to take it further. Although most people would be happy with a small amount of honey or even just the pure enjoyment and serenity following the act of beekeeping, for me it seemed like the next step was to learn about Beehive Alchemy.

Bees always seemed to defy the laws of science with their ability to create things like honey, wax, and propolis. I held a deep admiration for these tiny creatures and wanted to dive deeper into my relationship with them. The burning question in my mind was, "Where do they get all of this from?" Initially, I satisfied my curiosity by simply observing their activities within the beehive. From making honeycomb to capping it off, and finally producing rich golden honey, I was mesmerized by their intricate processes. Little did I know that this precious substance would become the driving force behind my lifelong passion.

For thousands of years beekeeping has been about beekeepers maintaining their hives, and the fate of the bees themselves is almost unknown. In more recent centuries, beekeeping has been more about growing and marketing honey, resulting in some strange practices that have extended their lives and made them useless to their queen. The Beehive Alchemy class will introduce you to a new way of looking at things.

This is about defining the things that are important to you, and how to begin letting go of the things that no longer serve you.

This chapter is about helping others realize their potential, and then channeling that awareness into a tangible form.

As alchemy will teach you, everything is changeable. You cannot hold on to things permanently because they eventually change in their intrinsic properties and therefore become irrelevant.

Chapter 1
Alchemy and Beeswax In The Beehive

What is beeswax?

Candle making requires beeswax as a crucial ingredient. Without beeswax, we would not have the pleasure of lighting beeswax candles. In fact, you probably wouldn't be reading about the process of making them. One unique quality of beeswax is its natural scent of delicious honey. Despite this, many individuals are not familiar with beeswax and its uses. This section aims to educate people on this versatile substance.

In simple words, beeswax is an organic material which is produced by the female worker honey bees through the glands found under their belly. This secretion is commonly called beeswax scale. The average width of the scale is about three millimeters, and it usually is irregular in shape. Each gram of beeswax needs about two thousands of these beeswax scales to be made. So, the amount of wax needed for an average beeswax candle comes from about a million beeswax scales. If the scales are smaller than average which does happen at times, then this number can be significantly larger.

Intrinsically, beeswax is white in color or see through; this is based on how thick the scales are. The thickness of the scales produced by the bees depends on their age. Bees that are young or old produce slim scales, whereas the middle-aged ones produce dense scales.

For the secretion of wax to take place, the temperature of the hive needs to be approximately ninety-seven degrees Fahrenheit. It is observed that the rate of wax production witnesses a rise during the months of April to June, due to the queen's endeavor to repopulate the colony and consequent surplus flow of nectar. This happens to be the precursor to honey. Most experts believe that, due to the massive deluge of honey being produced, bees step up their scale production to make more room to store the honey made.

There are four species of honeybees out there in the world; however, most of the man-made products utilize the beeswax produced by a species called Apis mellifera. The remaining species of bees produce meager amounts of beeswax, including honey, and are difficult to work with; hence, they are not preferred.

A surprising fact of which most people are unaware is that bees need to consume honey to make the scales. Research has indicated variations in the amount of honey consumed; however, on an average, about eight to ten portions of honey goes into producing a single unit of beeswax. Bees which are producing wax do not engage in any other work apart from the secreting. Once the wax is secreted, it is the worker bees' responsibility to amass them into honeycomb.

The shape of the honeycomb cells is believed to be hexagonal because of the rigidity it offers in comparison to other shapes. These honeycombs are used to hoard both the honey and the larvae of the bees.

Although beeswax candles come in multitudes of colors, the actual color of the beeswax varies on its origin and hygiene. Beeswax from infected hives is usually brownish in color and are unfit for use. It has been observed that beeswax with brownish tinge often have chemicals in them owing to their origins, and so such beeswax is sold cheap. The premium quality beeswax is either cream or white in color. However, this color is not natural and results from chemical refining. Beeswax is naturally gold in color due to the nectar and pollen stored in them.

Once the comb is full of honey, it is covered with white beeswax upon ripening. Most beeswax candle makers return the honeycomb to the bees once they are done with it. The candles are exclusively made from the new hygienic beeswax taken from the outermost honeycomb cells, post the extraction of honey.

In terms of chemical elements, beeswax comprises of at least two hundred and eighty-four constituents. On the contrary, pure beeswax comprises of only oxygen, hydrogen and carbon. It has been found that, the sweet fragrance of honey originates from only about fifty of the constituents found in beeswax. The beeswax is not directly used; it is cleaned and refined for hygiene reasons.

Applications of Beeswax

The many uses of beeswax have been documented for centuries, from the ancient myths of Icarus using beeswax wings to the supposed healing powers of Pilyn's broth. It is clear that beeswax has been valued and utilized long before the present day. In fact, certain cultures even used it as a form of currency. The Romans are said to have demanded ten thousand pounds of beeswax as a tax when they conquered Corsica, while French farmers were required to pay an annual tax of two pounds in the 1300s. This demonstrates the high value placed on beeswax in earlier times. It is also worth noting that during this period, the Catholic Church in Rome mandated the use of beeswax candles for prayers and other religious services, further emphasizing its significance. Although centuries have passed since then, beeswax continues to be used for various purposes today, which includes:

As a lubricant

Most people do not realize that beeswax is an excellent lubricant. It is especially used to oil old furniture joints. In addition to furniture joints, it can also be used to smoothen the movement of windows and doors.

As a Mustache Cream

A good number of mustache creams use beeswax as the key ingredient. By applying these creams, men can harden their mustaches and shape it as they wish. It can easily be made at home, provided that some beeswax is accessible. All it requires is just melting of about eight ounces of beeswax in a Bain Marie (a type of double boiler). Then, mix it with four ounces of petroleum jelly. It is ready to be used after the mixture cools.

To preserve the metal articles

Moisture in the air is responsible for the tarnishing of bronze articles. In order to keep the moisture from making contact with the surface of the bronze, a solution of beeswax and turpentine may be applied on the surface. This sticks to the surface as a protective coat. Applying molten beeswax on the surface of copper is found to protect it. Also, most iron articles are coated with beeswax to prevent rusting.

Lubing for jewelry making

Most people do not know that jewelers often use beeswax for lubing purposes, such as when carving intricate strands from precious metals like gold and silver.

As a glazing agent

A lot of cheese makers utilize beeswax for glazing purposes in order to protect the cheese from contamination. Although plastic was used for some time, it was found that it imparted an unpleasant zest to the cheese. It is not used any longer for this reason.

As a wood conditioner

An excellent wooden conditioner can be prepared by heating a mixture comprising of one part of edible inorganic oil and five parts beeswax. The ratios of beeswax and oil may be varied to get a thicker paste if needed. It is commonly used to condition wooden articles like bowls and boards.

To tackle oil spills

Most people are unaware that NASA uses a blend of beeswax and some enzymes to eliminate cases of oil spillage. The beeswax absorbs all of the oil, while the enzymes decompose it. This can be utilized to clear oil spills in oceans as well.

To make sweets

Fruit gums, jellybeans, and other sweets, such as toffees, are fabricated from beeswax. Beeswax gives these sweets their texture and holds all the flavor without allowing it to get debilitated.

For protection of leather

People take great care to ensure that their expensive leather does not come in contact with water. One of the best ways to protect leather from water is to apply a smelted mixture of beeswax with tallow and neat's-foot oil all in equivalent ratios.

To polish Granite

Molten beeswax is the best polish for granite counters, for it cleans it up like magic. It is spread evenly on the granite surface and intended to be used as a polish. Then, after some time, it is wiped with a smooth piece of cloth. The surface will get its sheen back like it is brand new.

Materials required

We are going to discuss the process of rendering beeswax. It is a single stage purification procedure; there is no need to filter again and again. Most of the processes for rendering beeswax require melting the beeswax more than once; this makes it cumbersome and time consuming. Most of the other rendering methods are slight variations of the crude method of rendering beeswax. We are going to discuss the process of rendering, which is way more efficient than the crude methods or its variants. In this section, we shall list all the items required to render beeswax efficiently.

The list of items needed to render beeswax are:

A sizable old container which can withstand heat, since traces of wax are likely to stick on to it after the rendering. It is recommended to use some old, disposable container.

- A good quality cheesecloth which has a high thread count. The higher the thread count, the more suited it is to this procedure.

- Some tight cloth clips or pegs, preferable made out of plastic, so that they do not get heated up easily.

- Amassed beeswax which is as clean as possible

- Long metal tongs with sufficient width for gripping them tightly.

Rendering beeswax from the honeycomb

The procedure of rendering beeswax from honeycomb takes about forty to forty-five minutes to complete. This excludes the time for it to cool off. The procedure we are about to discuss is a single stage refinement procedure.

One of the crude methods of rendering beeswax involves melting it directly in a container of water after which the impurities are removed through a strainer. This is followed by pouring it through a filter paper to get rid of all the micro impurities. The filtering process is repeated many times till the beeswax is refined to the maximum extent possible. This process is both cumbersome and time-consuming. We are going to discuss a far simpler and more efficient method to render beeswax.

Step 1: Firstly, a large strip of cheesecloth is spread on a plane area. Next, pieces of honeycomb are placed right in the middle of the cheesecloth. You don't need to worry if the honeycomb contains impurities like larva or dead bees embedded within it. It will get segregated eventually as the process continues. Finally, the cheesecloth is tied up into a bundle, such that all of the honeycomb pieces are close together inside the cheesecloth. In case the bundle is too large and likely to come open, it can only be fastened by means of cloth clips. It is time to move on to the next step once a snug bundle is prepared.

Step 2: A large container which can hold the cheesecloth bundle well inside is filled with water and kept on the stove. After this, the cheesecloth bundle is placed inside the container with the water. The burner is ignited, while the flame intensity is kept at a medium. Eventually, when the water boils, the beeswax from the honeycomb will melt down and permeate out of the cheesecloth. The impurities that were in the honeycomb will continue to remain inside the cheesecloth. You can observe the melted beeswax floating as a yellow liquid in the water. For best results, it is recommended that the cheesecloth (which is used to hold the honeycomb) will have multiple layers. The beeswax then melts out and will be even more pure. Better filtration will be achieved with the additional number of layers.

Step 3: After almost all the wax seems to have melted out of the bundle, it is time to force the trace amount of beeswax still left in the bundle out into the water. This step will ensure that the maximum possible amount of beeswax has been extracted from the honeycomb. It is recommended the squeezing process to be done with a pair of tongs, since the cheesecloth bundle is likely to be hot in this stage. The cheesecloth bundle may be twisted or pressed or wrung in as many ways possible, so that the maximum amount of beeswax is extracted.

Step 4: The cheesecloth bundle can be taken out of the container after the previous step. The container with the melted wax and water mixture is then allowed to cool. The cooling process may take hours. The beeswax will gradually condense into a thick layer on the top of the water. Once the cooling is complete, the layer of beeswax will solidify as it floats on the water. It will take on a darker shade of yellow color once it solidifies. You need not worry, for if there are some bubbles in the beeswax, they will disappear once it completely solidifies.

Step 5: Once the beeswax has completely solidified, it can be easily taken out of the container by pressing on the edges of the lump of beeswax. It should easily come out of the container without any issues. After the beeswax is taken out of the container, it should be laid on a clean cloth to remove the water remaining on the surface. After it is completely dried out, you have a pure lump of cleaned beeswax extracted from the honeycomb.

Purification of the beeswax

While beeswax candles can be easily obtained from the store, there is a sense of satisfaction in creating them at home. Some may not know that beeswax candles are powerful air purifiers, releasing negatively charged ions into the atmosphere that bind with positively charged pollutants like dust and pollen. This process, called negative ionization, clears viruses and bacteria from the air. Unlike paraffin candles, which emit harmful fumes, beeswax candles are a healthier option. Making homemade candles may seem daunting, but it's actually quite simple - just make sure to purify the beeswax before use.

Obtaining good quality raw beeswax for candles is not exactly an easy process. That is why it is essential to purify the beeswax before it is made out into candles. No matter what kind of candles are going to be made from of the beeswax, be it scented candles or colored beeswax candles, the process of purifying it is absolutely essential. Most people do not realize that unprocessed beeswax consists of fragments of propolis and other wastes which are not suitable for candle making. This section hopes to shed some light on this aspect, since a lot of people are unaware on how to do it efficiently.

Firstly, the supplies needed for this process need to be kept handy. It requires a double boiler, a finely knit item of clothing - such as a pillow cover, some parchment paper, and a large, heat-resistant container.

Step 1: The beeswax needs to be emptied onto the double boiler. You can utilize a steel bowl in the absence of a double boiler, placing it inside a container containing boiling water. The beeswax is made to melt thoroughly in the container, such that it turns into a total liquid. The process of melting can take some time; however, acceleration may cause sudden overflow. The melting process should be done on a medium heat and must be supervised for safety reasons.

Step 2: Next, the bowl is lined with parchment paper in order to serve as mold for the hot wax when it is poured into the bowl. The fine knit cloth is lined over this parchment paper. The piping hot wax is poured into the bowl once the lining part is complete. The cloth is then lifted off the bowl so that all the waste, including propolis, is segregated from the wax. The cloth should be held over the bowl until the hot wax stops dripping. The hot beeswax should be allowed to cool slowly. The cooling process should happen naturally without any external aid so that it settles well. After it has solidified, the wax hunk can be easily removed by yanking on the parchment paper. The melted beeswax may also be poured into silicon molds after it is purified. This just makes the process of cleaning up after easier. This process can be repeated to further purify the beeswax as needed. The number of times the purification needs to be repeated depends on the source of the beeswax. Cleaner beeswax is usually more expensive. Once the beeswax is thoroughly purified, then it can be used to make immaculate candles.

Although the purification process is not exactly that difficult, cleaning up the bowl after the whole process can be messy. However, there is a trick in order to simplify the cleanup post the filtering. For this, the wax-stained bowl is heated to about two hundred degrees Fahrenheit in the oven. After the heating is over, the traces of wax should melt down into liquid which can be easily cleaned with the help of tissue papers. Once the traces of wax are removed, do not forget to wash it neatly with plenty of soap and water.

Chapter 2
Alchemy For The Body

The majority of the cures presented in this chapter are historical or widely employed. Their usefulness is determined by scientists and physicians, because they have scientific validity. The recipes presented here are not meant to be taken as gospel, but rather as a way of using these ancient medicines to improve your own health and well-being. It is your choice whether to utilize them or not.

In the Beehive Alchemy class, we will focus on the animals of the world and their uses for rejuvenation of the body, so that you may rekindle your own love for life in pursuit of this ancient philosophy.

Alchemy for the body is about rejuvenating your own physical health. Using traditional medicines, you can improve your overall well-being and live a healthier life.

The real benefit of this section is to awaken within you a respect for the herbs and insects that were once revered and used extensively throughout history in order to improve one's own health, or that of others.

purity

When using goods from your own bees, you can rest assured that they are pure, unadulterated, and authentic. This is because they were made the way they are supposed to be made.

When making your own products, you can rest assured that they are pure because they were made with love, knowledge and respect.

When alchemists use their bees as tools to help them achieve their goal, they realize a deeper purpose regarding protection of the bees and their hive. When you give your bees a certain job or task, you are also realizing something important about yourself and your relationship with them.

Recently, it was discovered that some "pure honey" marketed by big supermarkets in the United Kingdom is not exactly what it purports to be. It has been found that the honey, which is said to come from local British suppliers, actually comes from China. Pure beeswax has been found in some of these "honey" products. One supplier was fined a total of £70,000 for selling adulterated honey.

The premise of alchemy is about bringing the world into harmony with itself and with nature by creating a balance.

If your bees do not produce enough or any honey and you need honey, your local farmers market may have any of the materials that you need to fulfill your needs. This is also true for any other products that are not readily available.

When you produce your own beeswax or honey, you realize that it is possible to give a gift to yourself and your family. This is the first step to establishing a balance in your life, and any order that you introduce into the world will eventually be returned to you in kind.

Before continuing, never offer honey to infants younger than 12 months or adults with serious allergies.

It was found that the pollen from the Hockney-Friesian breed is one of the most potent bee pollens. This is a good strain for those who are new to beekeeping because it protects against mites, has a long flowering season and produces good honey crops.

In order to maintain an optimum level of health, make sure you obtain pure beeswax, honey and propolis for your own consumption or for formulation of your own personal beeswax products.

Soothing sunburn – Honey is excellent in hydrating and defending the skin. Honey and aloe vera can be combined to form a soothing treatment for sunburns. It will aid in reducing the inflammation and redness.

Lip care – If your lips are chapped, honey can restore their health. It will heal, hydrate, and calm. Simply apply a small amount, or if you have more time, you may prepare an incredible lip balm by combining honey, beeswax, coconut oil, a touch of lemon essential oil, and vitamin E oil.

Cold care – Honey can assist with sore throats and congestion. Additionally, it can be a wonderful pick-me-up for those who are unable to eat due to illness. Mix it with hot water, lemon, and cinnamon to create a calming drink that will help you fight off the common cold.

Honey is utilized for cosmetic treatments due to its natural characteristics.

Facial mask – Use five parts honey to one part apple cider vinegar. Massage into the skin and leave for up to 15 minutes before rinsing with warm water.

Hair treatment – Apply a mixture of honey, ripe banana, and coconut oil on wet hair. It helps restore the beauty of damaged hair if left on for up to 15 minutes before rinsing.

Scar treatment – Combine equal parts honey and coconut oil. Cover the scar with a warm washcloth until it has cooled. Repeat every day. This has been demonstrated in certain studies to diminish the look of scars.

Pore cleaner – Honey and coconut oil are combined in a 2:1 ratio. Apply to skin and allow to sit for a few minutes prior to rinsing. To generate a natural exfoliator, coffee, flaxseed, or ground oats can be added to the mixture.

Rough or cracked skin treatment – When dry and cracked, apply honey directly to the heels, elbows, palms, etc. After allowing it to sit for several minutes, remove it using a warm washcloth. Especially beneficial during the dry winter months.

Bee pollen

As promised, let's revisit the topic of bee pollen. In our previous discussion, we covered how to gather and store it. The end result is small crunchy pellets that can be easily added to drinks, yogurt, cereal, or smoothies. Recent research has revealed that these tiny grains have similar antioxidant effects to those found in fermented foods. Some beekeepers suggest using bee pollen as a way to boost immunity against seasonal allergies since it contains pollens from the surrounding area. The German Federal Board of Health has recognized bee pollen as a stand-alone medicine. It is marketed as a superfood with potential benefits such as anti-inflammatory properties, antioxidant properties, liver support, immune system enhancement, nutritional supplementation, relief from menopause symptoms, stress reduction, and accelerated wound healing.

propolis

Prior to this, we examined propolis, the resin-like substance produced by bees. This appears to have anti-inflammatory properties as well as other therapeutic properties. People have been known to use it to cure diabetes, cold sores, inflammation, and burns, among other ailments.

Manuka

Manuka honey is a honey that appears to be more adaptable than any other. The manuka plant is the same species from which tea tree oil is extracted, and tea tree oil's medicinal benefits are well-known. The manuka plant, or Leptospermum scoparium to use its Latin name, is native to south-eastern Australia and New Zealand.

Technically, any of us could create manuka honey if we had a five-mile radius of manuka bushes and positioned our beehives in the center, because the most frequent plant influences the composition of our honey.

This manuka honey possesses antimicrobial, anti-inflammatory, and antioxidant properties. In addition, it includes methylglyoxal, an antibacterial compound whose benefits beyond those of regular honey. It is believed to arise from the conversion of dihydroxyacetone, which is particularly concentrated in manuka flower nectar. Considering this, manuka honey is lauded for possessing characteristics superior to those of regular honey.

There appears to be no limit to the fantastic applications of bee products. We as natural beekeepers will eventually benefit from the possibility to gather these items, even though we are not mainly focused on doing so. It is the icing on the cake, considering all the good we are doing for our habitats and the planet's ecology.

Chapter 3
Alchemy Candle

The first candles looked different from the ones we use today. The old candles were torches, made from reeds core and soaked in animal fats. The fat kept the light on and slowed the burning of the reed's core. They were called "rushlights" and not candles.

It was only in 3000 B.C. that candles took some shape and form. The ancient Egyptians were the first to be documented to create the candles that we know. They were the first to make wicked candles. The Egyptians created wicked candles by repeatedly dipping the tiny, rolled papyrus in melted beeswax or tallow (animal fat). They discovered that the wick takes a certain form when the beeswax or tallow hardened. The new type of candle can stand and lasts longer.

Candles redeemed its popularity again in the late 20th century. In the 1980's, it became popular as a decoration. It was marketed in different designs, sizes, colors, shapes and scents. It was used to improve the ambiance in homes, offices and restaurants.

Different waxes were also discovered in the same decade. The new waxes are more affordable and safer. It was easier to handle, mold and design. This allowed creativity to be incorporated in candle makings. It opened the surge of artistic and beautiful affordable candles.

In the early 21st century, different uses of candles were also discovered. Herbs and other essential oils were added to the candle, so they can be used as scented candles for aromatherapy, wellness and romantic purposes.

Today, handmade candles are more popular and are becoming a good home business for homemakers.

Steps of Candle Making

There are 4 main processes that you need to know in candle making. These processes may determine the consistency, strength and burn time of your candle. Below is the list of the 4 essential processes:

1. **Wax melting**. The wax needs to be correctly melted in order to produce strong and beautiful candles.

2. **Wicking the candle**. Your wick may become submerged in the wax if you do not know how to place or hold the wick.

3. **Pouring of the wax**. You may think that pouring of the wax does not require a technique or process, but it does. If you pour the wax wrongfully, your candles may have sinkholes near the wick. It may affect the strength and stability of your candles.

4. **Curing**. This is the process of making the wax harden. You can cure the wax naturally by leaving it at room temperature overnight. Or you may place it in the fridge or freezer. But not all wax may be cured in the freezer or fridge.

Additional processes may be needed between the basic processes, depending on the kind of candles you are making. Some of these processes are dependent on the additives of your candles.

Melting the Wax

Determining the amount of wax needed

Before you could melt the wax, you may have to undergo an additional process. This is about how to determine how much wax you should melt. Candle making kits have already pre-measured the wax you need. But, if you want to start making candles for business, you should familiarize yourself with this process.

This process will help you save some of your wax. Here are the steps:

1. *Weigh your mold*.

2. *Fill your mold with water and take the weight*.

3. *Subtract the weight of the mold from the total weight of the mold and the water*. The difference is the amount of wax you need.

For example: Your mold weighs 1 ounce. When you weighed it with water, the result is 7 ounces. Therefore, you need six ounces of wax.

4. Every pound of solid wax yield different amount of melted wax. Here are the approximate amount of each type of wax when melted:

a. Paraffin wax. 1 pound can yield 18 to 20 ounces.

b. Soy wax. 1-pound yields 16 ounces.

c. Beeswax. 1-pound yields 14 ounces.

d. Palm wax. 1 pound may yield 14 to 16 ounces.

e. Gel wax. 1 pound may yield 16 ounces.

Melting techniques

There are many ways to melt the wax. If you are only using a small amount of wax, you may melt it in the microwave.

If you are using soft waxes like soy wax and beeswax, you may melt it by steaming or double boiling.

The best way to melt paraffin wax and other hard waxes is through a double boiler. You may also melt it through direct heat, but the wax may collect carbon and may have black bits.

Below are the steps to follow when melting the wax through a double boiler. This book only covers this type of process because it is the basic melting process you need for candle-making.

1. Prepare two pots of different sizes.

2. Fill the bigger pot with water at around 1 inch deep. Place it over medium heat and bring to a soft boil.

3. While you are waiting for the water to boil, prepare the amount of wax you need. Put it in the smaller pot. If you have a clip thermometer, or if you can clip your thermometer in the smaller pot, put it in.

4. After all the wax had totally melted, check its temperature. Make sure that the temperature is at 180 degrees Fahrenheit. Turn off the stove and leave the wax to cool a little (about 90 to 135 degrees) for the pouring process.

Adding Additives and Wicking

Prior to the pouring process, there may be three steps that you need to do. These are adding fragrance and essential oils, wicking the candle, and decorating the candle.

Adding Fragrance Oil

Since fragrance oils can affect the consistency and stability of the wax, the process may overlap with the process of melting the wax. Here are the steps when adding the oil:

1. Decide how much fragrance oil you want to add or know how much oil is required by the recipe.

2. Determine the weight of the fragrance oil. Because of the different consistency, an ounce of oil and an ounce of melted wax may have different volume. Thus, base your additional wax on the weight of the oil and not according to its volume.

For example: You intend to use 1 ounce of lemon cheesecake fragrance oil. Some manufacturers produce it in syrup form, which has a thicker consistency than the wax. One fluid ounce of the fragrance oil may weigh more than one fluid ounce of melted wax.

3. Prepare the same weight of wax and add it to the original amount of wax before proceeding with the melting process.

4. During the cooling period, prior to the pouring process, mix in your fragrance oil.

5. Proceed with the pouring process.

Adding Essential Oils

Essential oils are added before the pouring process. But you need to test the scent of the oil before the pouring process because some oils lose their scent or emit a foul scent when heated.

Here are the steps when adding essential oils:

1. After the wax had melted, add 10 drops of your desired essential oil to the wax. If the essential oil retains its smell, then wait for the pouring process.

2. If the essential oil does not retain its smell, you can add more drops of the essential oil to the wax until the wax become scented.

3. Let the wax cool a little for the pouring process.

4. After the wax had cooled, check if the scent remained. If it did, then proceed with the pouring process. If it did not, add a little more of the essential oil before pouring.

Adding Herbs and Spices

Since there are two ways of adding herbs in your candle, the steps for each may differ from each other.

Adding Dry Herbs Directly to the Candle

• If you are adding crushed dried herbs, you can add it directly to the wax after the cooling down period for the pouring process.

• If you are adding spices, but you want the powder to be visible, add it before the pouring process. If you do not want it to be visible, add it after the wax had melted.

• If you are adding herbs, spices and dried flowers as side decors for pillars or votive candles, then you may have to do the following steps:

1. After the wax had cooled a little, take a small amount of the wax.

2. Brush the sides of your molds with the wax.

3. Place the mold in the fridge for about a minute or until the wax had set.

4. Add another coat of wax. Arrange your herbs, dried leaves or flowers at the side of your mold.

5. Brush another coat of wax over the herbs. Repeat step 3.

6. Repeat step 5 twice.

7. Wait for the pouring process.

• If you are adding spices, herbs and flowers as a design for container candles, you may follow the steps mentioned above. But if you want them to have a floating effect, you may add them during the pouring process.

Adding herbal essences by infusion

To infuse your candle with herbs, just add the herbal flowers, leaves, root or bark in the oil after the melting process. Leave the herbs in the wax until it cools for the pouring process.

Strain the herbs before pouring the wax into the container or mold.

Adding Dyes

The steps in adding essential oil to the candle are also the same for adding dyes. But, instead of the scent, the basis is the color of the wax.

Wicking the Candle

There are two ways of wicking your candle. You can wick it using a wick pin and wick holder. But you can do without both.

If you are using wick pins and wick holders, you may follow these steps.

1. Attach your wick to the wick pin or tab. Place the wick with a pin at the center of your mold or container. For container candles, you may permanently attach the bottom end of the wick with a glue gun or candle round stickers.

2. Insert the other end of the wick to the wick holder.

3. Arrange the wick holder on the top of the mold or the container. Make sure that the wick is centered.

4. Pour the wax in the mold or container. Adjust the wick to the center.

5. Leave the wick holder until the wax hardens.

6. Slowly remove the wick holder and trim the excess wick.

If you are not using a pin or holder, you can wick your candle by using skewers or toothpicks as holder. But this process is only advisable for cored wicks or HTP series wicks.

The steps are simple. Just tie the wick in the skewer or toothpick. Place the improvised wick holder on top of the mold or the container. Make sure to pour the wax slowly so the wick will remain at the center.

*Note: In wicking your candle, make sure to follow the steps in choosing the right wick for your candles.

Pouring the Wax

Except if you are adding designs to your candle, the steps in pouring the wax to your mold or container remains the same. Here are the steps:

1. After the wax had melted, cool your wax until the temperature drops to around 90 to 135 degrees. You must let your wax cool down or it will make your wax float.

2. Give the wax a slow stir to burst any bubbles.

3. Pour the wax into the container. In pouring, start at the center or near the wick, especially if you are using an unwaxed wick. The wick will absorb the wax near it and may result in a sinkhole in the middle.

4. Fill the mold or the container up to three fourths of its height.

5. Lightly cure the candle by leaving it at room temperature for four hours or by putting it in the fridge for at least an hour. Do not freeze the wax or else, the wax will not sink and will not cover possible sinkholes.

6. After the light cure, reheat the remaining wax. Pour it on top of the hardened candle until you covered the mold or the desired limit for the container.

7. Let the candle cure at room temperature for at least 8 hours before lighting it.

Curing the Candle

The curing process only has one step and that is to leave the candle for at least 8 hours at room temperature. Some candles may require longer curing period.

There is also a process of fast cure. This is putting the newly poured candle in the fridge to cure faster.

Removing the Candle from the Mold

If you are using reusable mold, one challenge that you may encounter is removing the candles from the mold. Incorrect unmolding may result to cracked or broken candles. There are two steps that can make it easy for you to overcome this hurdle. The first one is seasoning your mold and the other is shrinking the wax.

- **Seasoning.** This is the process of making the mold in tune with the wax you are using. This could mean that you may have to use a specific mold for every wax you use. This process can take a while, too.

To season your mold, just melt the wax and pour into the mold. Let the wax harden. Take out the hardened wax from the mold. You may notice that some bits of the wax may be left behind or the wax will have some dent.

Melt the wax again and pour it back to the mold. Then repeat the previous step.

Continue to repeat the steps until the wax comes out clean and almost perfect. This will now make it easier for you to unmold your candles.

- **Shrinking.** It is the process of shrinking the candle in the fridge or freezer.

If the candle would not slip out of the mold, do not tap the mold. You may dent or break the wax. Instead, place the mold in the fridge for five minutes or in the freezer for a minute.

The wax will shrink, and the candle will become smaller. It will slip easily out of the mold.

Designing the Candle

Between some of the processes, the candle can be decorated. Chapter 6 of this book will teach you some simple, but elegant designs for your candles.

Dipped Candles

These candles are exquisite to look at and are artistic in nature. They are long, cylindrical, tube-like candles that have a narrowing snout at the top. They are generally seen in an array of colors. They are also known as dipped tapers.

These are made primarily using beeswax and paraffin wax. With that said, you can also use soy wax to create dipped tapers. However, should you intend to do that, it is good to know that the soy wax will need a longer set up time between the layers. For this example, you can work with either the beeswax or the paraffin wax.

The reason why beeswax is used more commonly to create these tapers is the fact that melted beeswax is more viscous. This means that you will need to do less 'dipping', as compared to paraffin wax. You may only need to dip it between seven to 10 times, whereas for the paraffin, you will need to dip twice as much. It is also to be noted that the beeswax tapers burn a little longer, as opposed to their paraffin counterparts.

In case you are on a tighter budget, you can always opt to use paraffin as your choice of wax. It will take a lot more dipping than the beeswax to achieve the kind of thickness you are looking for. However, you can rest assured that you will still end up with exquisite results using paraffin. For paraffin users, it is preferred that you use straight paraffin with a medium or high melting point. Some types of paraffin wax melt at lower temperatures, so those are the kind you should avoid.

You can find some types of paraffin wax with medium melting points and should be able to take advantage of the hardening additives. These would give your tapers a more rigid look and feel. One of the most common hardening additives found in paraffin wax is called stearic acid, also known as stearine. Whatever you choose between the beeswax or the paraffin, you can achieve the desired results.

The Materials

To create the dipped candles, you will need:

- Beeswax or paraffin
- Double boiler
- Wick of your choice
- Wick pins
- Thermometer
- Cold water
- A broom
- Mat knife

You do not need any additional items to make dipped candles.

The Method

Step One

Start by setting up your double boiler, then place the wax of your choice in it to start the melting process. Once the wax is melted, transfer it into a pot. You will need to use a tall pot, ideally of the height you wish your candles to achieve. You can place this pot in a stockpot that is half-full of water. Place the stockpot over high heat.

With a thermometer, keep checking the temperature and ensure that it remains under 200 degrees. Ideally, the working temperature should be around 165 degrees.

Step Two

This step is a bit tricky, but with a bit of practice, you should soon be able to do this relatively easy.

You will need to create a rig that can hold the length of the wick. Depending on the size of your taper, you will need to use a wick twice the length of the taper. This is necessary because you will need to dip your tapers in pairs. Ensure that you do not make your tapers taller than the dipping vat you are using.

Step Three

You will also need to tie some weights at the wick ends. For that, you can use metal nut fishing weights, or even a few coins stuck together (use a bit of wax). The weights are used to ensure that the wicks are held straight and are taut. Do not worry, as you will be cutting these off around halfway through the process.

Once your wicks have started to accumulate some wax, they will remain straight on their own.

Step Four

Start dipping your tapers. You can continue to repeat the process until you have acquired the desired thickness. You will need to allow several minutes for the layers to cool off before you apply another one on them. If you do not allow these layers to cool off properly, the wax will start to fall off the wick.

Ensure that the dipping motion is continuous and smooth. You will also need to make sure that you do not pause when the tapers are submerged.

Step Five

When you have achieved around half of the thickness you desire, cut off the weights at the bottom of the tapers. Continue dipping your tapers a few more times. After having reached the desired thickness, just hang your tapers and let them dry.

Note: Always make sure that you use a scale and measure out the thickness/diameter of the taper holders, and then measure the thickness of your tapers to ensure the correct thickness is achieved.

It is a good practice to leave your newly created tapers to hang as a pair. It is easier for storage purposes, and each taper acts as a counterbalance to the other, allowing both to remain steady and straight. Once they have cooled off, simply cut the connecting wick and use them as you please.

Using Molds

Molded candles are wonderful gifts and very fun to make! You can make candles in practically any shape you can think of. These whimsical crafts are beautiful to look at and can be scented with anything you wish.

When it comes to picking a mold, there is a huge variety of options. You can find candle molds in many different shapes and sizes. No matter what you go with, here are some tips:

- Metal molds are most common and easy to find and clean.

- You need a mold sealer to seal the wick hole before pouring in the wax.

- Don't screw the wick screw too tight, you might break the wick. The point of the wick screw is just to hold the wick in place, not seal the hole.

To make:

1. Melt, dye, and scent as with the basic candle recipe.

2. Run the wick through the wick hole on your mold and attach the other end to a wick stick so it doesn't fall.

3. Secure the wick in the wick hole, then add mold sealer to make sure the wax doesn't leak!

4. Pour wax into your mold (prepare as directed in the basic candle recipe). Keep some excess for the final step.

5. Once a surface has formed on your candle and it has begun to harden, poke some relief holes in the candle, this will accommodate the natural wax shrinkage.

    a. These holes should go around the wick (put about four of them in) and should be poked almost all the way through the candle, just 1 inch away from the bottom.

    b. You may have to re-poke these holes to keep them open as the candle continues to dry. We'll fill them in the next step.

6. Once your candle has cooled (up to 24 hours or more) and is back at room temperature, you can fill in the relief holes. Heat the excess wax to about 5o to 10o F hotter than the original temperature you pored at (this is the help the layers seamlessly melt together). Add it on the top of the candle and let dry.

7. Remove the wax screw and mold sealer, then slide your candle out of the mold. If it's cooled completely, it should come out easily. If not, put it in the fridge for 15 minutes or so and try again (this will finish the shrinking process). Trim the wick off the bottom of the candle and trim the top wick about ¼" from the wax.

You're done! Now you can share your creations with the world.

Candle Making Kits

A kit for manufacturing candles from beeswax is a fantastic way to get your idea off the ground quickly. Depending on how much material is included, the cost of these candle-making kits varies.

The greatest advantage of using kits is that you acquire all the necessary materials in a single purchase. This ensures you will not need to reorder materials to complete the project.

However, you are restricted to the colors and other components included in the box, and the final product may be more expensive.

Beeswax Pillar Candles

It is somewhat difficult to make pillar candles. This is owing to the high temperature at which beeswax burns in compared to the appropriate wick size.

Using a custom mold for a bee supply is the easiest and most foolproof way to create pillar candles. Always use the wick size specified. If you do not use the appropriate wick size, your candle-making endeavor will fail.

Rolled Beeswax Candles
Gather the Materials

Beeswax candles produce a soothing glow and a beautiful, sweet aroma. Rolled beeswax candles are the easiest candles to make at home. Since the wax does not need to be melted, no melting pot or burner is required, making this activity suitable for both adults and children.

Here's what you'll require:

- Some sheets of beeswax. They are typically available in sheets measuring 8 inches by 16 inches.

- Wick appropriate for a 1-inch candle that has been primed.

- A razor blade or a sharp knife.

- Appropriate cutting surface.

Cut the Wick

Cut the wick ¾–inch longer than the wax sheet after lay it out on a beeswax sheet. Cut the wick to about 8 ¾–inches if you're using an 8-inch sheet.

Tip

On both sides, you can leave ¾–inch of wick. Thus, if one end of the candle appears nicer than the other, either end can be made the candle's top.

Roll the Beeswax Sheet

Start rolling the candle by bending over about 1/8 inch of the wax after laying the wick along the edge of the sheet. Enclose the wick in this little channel. Press down firmly to ensure the wax is tight around the wick, working from one end to the other along the length of the wick. This is the only time the beeswax sheets should be pressed firmly.

Some individuals like to flip the wax over and bend the 1/8-inch channel along a counter or cutting board's corner. Either way, it works. All that is required is a clean, straight route (, or channel) for the wick.

Roll Slow and Straight

It's time to be delicate with the wax after pressing the wick firmly into the wax. You do not want to squeeze or deform the pattern of the honeycomb.

Roll the candle carefully and straight, ensuring that the ends are kept even.

Finish Rolling Your Beeswax Candle

Roll the sheet till it reaches the end. If you wish to make a double-thick candle, simply butt a second sheet of wax up to the end of the first sheet, join them together by pressing the two sheets together with your thumbnail, and keep rolling.

Press the final edge down onto the candle's side gently. It should result in a somewhat smooth edge. You can press down with your thumb or thumbnail. If you left wick on both ends, choose the best-looking end for the top, cut the lower wick off, and then trim the top wick to around ½–inch.

Take pleasure in the gorgeous light and exquisite aroma of your beeswax candle or assist your children in gift-wrapping the candles they've made.

Variations

You can expand out with variants on the same theme after you've made your first beeswax candle.

1. To produce a short candle, cut the beeswax sheet in half.

2. To produce a thin candle, trim a sheet of beeswax vertically.

3. For a tapered beeswax candle, cut the sheet on the diagonal before setting the wick.

4. Combine two different hues (, or colors) of beeswax in a single candle.

5. Tea lights can be made with beeswax and cookie cutters.

Chapter 4
Beeswax and Propolis Projects

Beeswax is a natural product made by honey bees. It is used in many different industries and has a wide range of uses. The most common use of beeswax today is in candles and cosmetics, but it has also been used historically for waterproofing items such as leather goods. Beeswax is also often included in cosmetics because it contains antibacterial properties that help to prevent acne breakouts on the skin.

Salve Beeswax

Salve beeswax is a type of wax that can be used in a variety of ways. It has a creamy, soothing texture and can be used on your skin as a moisturizer or all-natural salve. It's often mixed with other ingredients like oils and herbs to make your own homemade salves, balms, lip balms, or hand creams.

Scrub Beeswax

Beeswax is a great natural abrasive, and it can be used for many projects around the house. Use it to polish wood, metal and plastic; clean glass, windows, mirrors and chrome; remove rust from tools; or even clean the inside of your oven!

To use beeswax as an abrasive: *Melt the wax in a double boiler on low heat. *Fill an old sock with the melted wax (this will be your applicator). *Dip your applicator into hot water. The wax should stick to it when you pull it out. *Rub over whatever surface you want to polish or clean. *Let cool before storing away again.

Body Butter Beeswax

This is a great beeswax project for the beginner. It's simple to make and requires only four ingredients: beeswax, shea butter, coconut oil and almond oil. The beeswax can be in bars or chunks; you'll need about 8 ounces of either type for each batch of body butter. For extra soothing properties, add a few drops of vitamin E oil to your mixture before melting it over low heat on the stovetop (or double-boiler method) until it becomes clear again—this will take about 10 minutes if all of your ingredients are room temperature. Then whip everything together until it becomes creamy smooth!

To finish off your body butter with essential oils that complement the base notes in the oils you've chosen: orange blossom for sweet scents like vanilla bean or lavender; rosemary or sandalwood when creating fresh fragrances such as basil leaf/thyme; patchouli when making floral blends such as jasmine/ylang ylang; minty aromas like peppermint stick blend well with grapefruit/lemon grass blends etcetera...

Furniture Polish Beeswax

Beeswax furniture polish is easy to make and works on wood, metal and plastic.

It can be used on all types of furniture and it's a natural alternative to commercial polishes.

Pet Care Beeswax

Beeswax and Propolis are also great for pet care. Beeswax can be used to treat:

- Skin (beeswax for skin)
- Fur (beeswax for fur)
- Ears (beeswax for ears)
- Paws (beeswax for paws)
- Teeth (beeswax for teeth).

Beeswax Lip Balm (Lip Balm, Lip Gloss)

Beeswax lip balm and beeswax lip gloss are great for protecting your lips from the cold weather. The recipe is simple, requiring only two ingredients: beeswax and honey.

To begin making your own beeswax lip balm or beeswax lip gloss you'll need:

- 1/4 cup of melted beeswax (you can melt at 175 degrees F)
- 1 tablespoon of honey (use raw honey)

Lotion bars beeswax

Lotion bars are the perfect way to make a moisturizing body lotion. They're easy to make, they're very effective and they are easy to carry with you. Lotion bars are great for people who have sensitive skin because they don't leak or spill in your purse like traditional liquid lotions do.

Fix'n Wax Beeswax

Beeswax is a wax produced by honeybees in the hive of their hives to build combs and store honey, pollen and propolis. The wax is secreted from glands on the abdomen of worker bees and molded into shapes by special bees, called "pressers". The amount of wax per bee varies from 1/12 oz (1g) for workers to 4/12 oz (4g) for drones.

Cleaning: To clean your candle holders, dip them into warm water with a little dish soap added. Then rinse them off with warm water again. Dry thoroughly before putting away or reusing. If you're using glass jars for storage or gift giving (instead of votive holders), be sure that all odors are out before storing anything inside them!

Making Candle Holders: Start with an old cup or bowl that has seen better days...or buy one at a thrift shop! Paint it with acrylic craft paint if you want a fun new look, then glue pieces of fabric around the rim; cut holes in each piece so they'll sit flat atop your cup or bowl when stretched across its surface area – then secure all edges tightly with hot glue gun - set aside until completely dry before filling up jar with whatever goodies you'd like!

Beeswax candles are a great alternative to beeswax candles. Beeswax, wax and oil can be used to make beeswax candles. Beeswax candles are used for decoration and to make a pleasant smell.

Beeswax Food Wraps

Beeswax food wraps are made from beeswax and are used to wrap food. Beeswax food wraps keep your food fresh, preserve its flavor, and help prevent spoilage. It's simple to make your own beeswax food wrap using supplies you probably already have in your kitchen.

Beeswax is a natural ingredient that can be found at most health-food stores or online. You can use any type of waxed paper as well—just cut it into squares before folding into pockets. Use the honeycomb pattern of folding here: fold one corner diagonally across the square towards where you started at a 90-degree angle; then fold both corners on each side meeting those diagonal edges together; then fold up one end to meet the center crease; then tuck under the bottom flap so it will stay secure when wrapped around an object such as a bowl or container with handles for carrying out of doors where there are flying insects which might contaminate our foods if left uncovered during transport time periods lasting longer than normal storage times would allow otherwise--we don't want them falling off onto ground surfaces surrounding our homes either!

Preserve Decorative Leaves

- Use a glass jar with a tight-fitting lid. A small jar with a metal lid will work as well.

- Place a piece of fabric or tissue paper over the opening of the jar to protect your leaves from moisture. Add water to fill about halfway up the side of your preserved leaf, then close it tightly and keep it in a cool place for about two weeks before removing from its moist environment (this makes them last longer).

Lotions Creams and Balms (Foot Balm, Honey, Oats, Soap)

Beeswax and cream: Beeswax is a great moisturizer, but you may need to add some other ingredients to make it thick enough.

- 3 tablespoons of beeswax (preferred) or 2 tablespoons of beeswax plus 2 tablespoons of grated hard soap

Beeswax and balm: You can use any kind of oil for this type of balm, but it's best if the oil has a high melting point so that when your hands get too hot, your balm won't melt down into something runny. We like coconut oil for its mild scent and high melting point—it's one of the few oils that remains solid at room temperature!

Polishes and protectors (garden tools, dubbin, beeswax wood polish)

Beeswax polish is an excellent protective coating for wooden surfaces and garden tools. Beeswax dubbin is a popular beeswax paste used to polish and protect leather, shoes, boots and saddles. A beeswax wood polish is made from actual pieces of wax (the same stuff that makes up your furniture). You can make your own garden tool protectors with this recipe:

Beeswax Wood Polish

Melt about 2 ounces of beeswax in a pan on low heat. Add 1 teaspoon lemon juice and 1/8 teaspoon turpentine to the melted wax. Pour into a container that has been warmed in hot water until it's pliable so you can squeeze out the contents later on as needed throughout the year.

Art & crafts (traditional batik on fabric, traditional easter egg, beeswax candle bowls)

This section includes projects for the artist and craftsperson. For example, you'll learn how to create a traditional batik on fabric and a traditional easter egg using beeswax or propolis. You'll also discover several simple yet elegant candle bowls that can be made with beeswax instead of paraffin wax. We recommend that you read through this section before beginning your project so that you understand of the basic techniques involved in each project.

Beeswax Bug Bite and Sting Balm

How to Make a Beeswax Bug Bite & Sting Balm

- 1 cup (240 ml) beeswax pellets or grated beeswax

- 1/2 cup (120 ml) olive or almond oil (for beeswax balms only)

- 3 tablespoons grated beeswax, melted and cooled slightly if using the softer wax in recipes like this one (omit if you are making pure beeswax balm)

- 5-7 drops essential oils of your choice: peppermint, eucalyptus, lavender or tea tree for bug bites and stings; tea tree for diaper rash; lavender for rashes of all kinds. You can also use plain lanolin from New Zealand sheep wool as an alternative to lanolin from sheep's wool rather than using lanolin cream on children under two years old. You can buy it at pharmacies in Australia or online at Amazon U.S.

- The original recipe uses cocoa butter instead of olive oil which makes it firmer than mine did so I added 2 tbsp back into it but you could omit that ingredient altogether if you prefer a firmer balm.*

Beeswax Hair Pomade

Beeswax and propolis hair pomade is a great alternative to petroleum-based hair pomades. It has the same staying power but will not leave your hair feeling greasy or weighed down by build-up. Beeswax and propolis are all natural ingredients and can be used on any type of hair!

- Measure out two tablespoons of beeswax into a small pot (you may need to experiment with how much you prefer).

- Add one tablespoon of lanolin, which is an animal fat found in sheep's wool (or available online).

- Melt over low heat until it becomes liquid enough that you can stir it together easily.

◇◇◇

Natural Solid Perfume

You can make a solid perfume by combining beeswax and propolis with essential oils. This is a great project to try if you have a couple of newbies at home, because it's very easy to do and it's not too messy or time-consuming. You will need:

- 3 tablespoons of beeswax granules

- 2 teaspoons of propolis (1 teaspoon will be used in this project but keep the other half for another project!)

- 1 teaspoon essential oil (your choice), such as lavender or lemon balm

Beeswax Sunscreen

- **Beeswax sunscreen:** Add a tablespoon of beeswax to 1/4 cup of coconut oil, melt them together in a double boiler. Once melted add 2 tablespoons of shea butter and stir until blended. Pour into an empty container and set aside for later use.

- **Beeswax lotions bar:** Melt 1 ounce of beeswax per cup or less into water in a double boiler; you may need to do this step several times depending on your recipe. The amount will vary based on what type of lotion bars you wish to make but this is a good start if you want some hints on how much wax or oils are needed for your own recipes then just multiply those amounts by 5 (the number of cups it takes before being able to pour out the mixture) so that there's enough room left over at the top without spilling it as they cool down while working with them during each round before pouring out another batch onto parchment paper until every last drop has been used up!

- **Acorn floating candles:** Mix 4 teaspoons acorns with one tablespoon water until fully combined then add 1 teaspoon cinnamon powder before mixing again until smooth consistency forms (should be thick enough where there aren't any gaps between ingredients anymore). Pour mixture into glass jar(s), let sit overnight before lighting up!

Sunscreen Lotions Bar

You can also make a beeswax-coconut oil lotion bar or one with olive oil, almond oil, avocado oil, cocoa butter, shea butter and mango butter. The beeswax is the base and you add your favorite oils to it. Beeswax absorbs more quickly than petroleum jelly so it's great for those who want an immediate application of moisture.

You might want to try these recipes:

- Beeswax + coconut oil

- Beeswax + olive oil

- Beeswax + almond oil

With each one you'll need a double boiler (or a glass Pyrex measuring cup in hot water), 1 oz of beeswax pellets (available at health food stores), 2 tablespoons of carrier oils (such as sweet almond or grapeseed) and roughly equal amounts of natural colorants (e.g., cocoa powder).

Drawing Salve for Splinters

The first thing you need to know about drawing salve is that it's not a "drawing" as in "pulling out." It's actually called drawing because it pulls the splinter out of your skin by adhering onto its surface.

This salve is made with beeswax and propolis extract, which are both excellent for healing wounds and cuts—and they smell good too! The ingredients also help protect the area from infection while they're healing. All you have to do is apply some salve on top of the splinter where it enters your skin, let it sit for 15-20 minutes (or longer if possible), then remove gently by pulling outward slightly while firmly pressing down towards yourself over the area so that all parts of the splinter come out (especially important if there are multiple fragments). Repeat until all pieces are removed!

Beeswax Ornaments

Beeswax ornaments are easy to make and fun to share with family and friends. You can use any shape of mold, such as an egg, a star, or a heart. You can also make one large ornament by using a wreath form for your mold. The color of the beeswax will determine what shade your ornament turns out to be—yellowish-brown if you use yellow wax; white if you use white wax; dark brown if you use dark brown wax.

If you want more than just plain old beeswax, try adding some scents—lavender oil creates a sweet aroma while lemon oil adds freshness (use sparingly). You can also add glitter or food coloring before pouring into molds; we recommend staying away from red since it has too much pigment in it when added directly on top of melted wax.

After making these little beauties at home, there are plenty of ways to display them around the house: They look great hanging from trees during Christmas time but also work well as place settings for dinner parties (especially weddings) throughout the year!

Beeswax is a fascinating compound that has many uses. It can be used as a food wrap, in lotions and creams, to make candles and other decorative items. There are various ways you can use beeswax in your home or garden, but these are just some of the most popular ones!

conclusion

Beehive alchemy is more than just crafting pretty objects. It is a means of harnessing the power of nature to heal and make use of resources.

By practicing this ancient art, you can learn to create valuable and enjoyable items from seemingly nothing. This knowledge an be applied to all aspects of life, from work and relationships to health and spirituality. Once considered a science, alchemy has been used for centuries to transform materials into gold and improve the lives of many through healing practices. I hope that this book serves as a guide on your journey towards self-discovery and growth, rather than simply a collection of stories. The information shared on this site is meant to assist you in finding your own path towards betterment.

Book 3

Bee Business

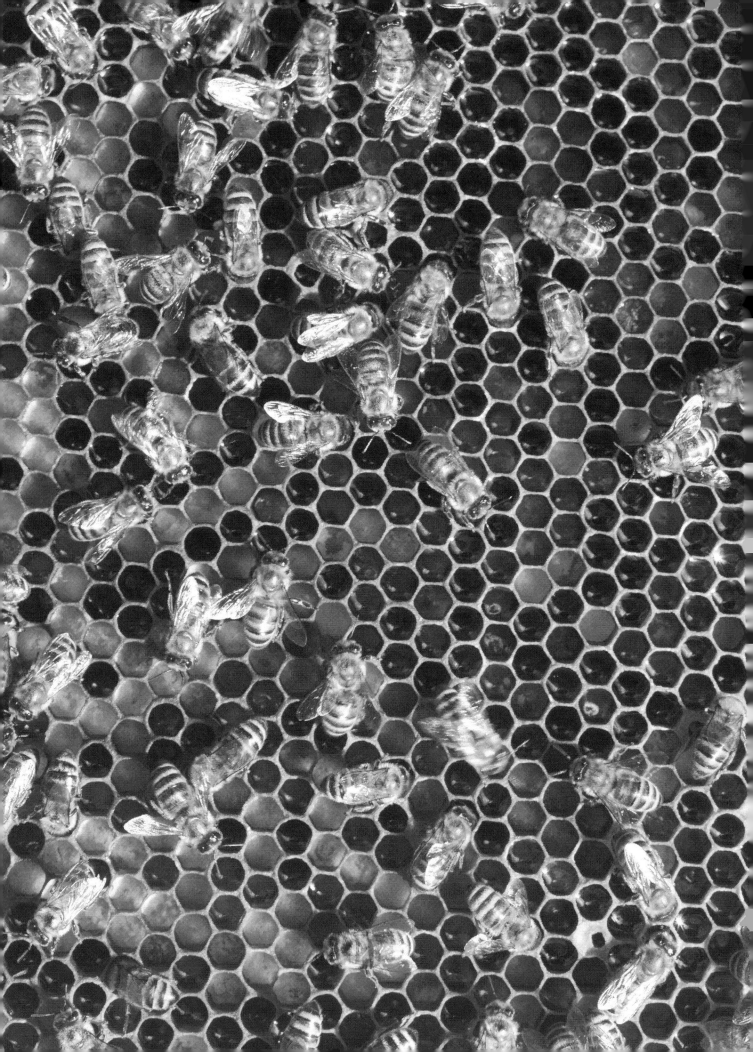

Introduction

Let's talk about the potential for a beekeeper to make money with their bees and beehives!

Beekeepers can make a lot of money if they know the right way to market their honey to earn a profit. Honey is very popular and an easy way for beekeepers to make money.

Here are the top three ways that beekeepers can earn additional revenue by marketing honey:

- Selling wholesale to local stores
- Selling online through e-commerce websites such as Amazon or Etsy
- Finding sponsors for your honey

The first step is to get the best beehives for space that you will need for your operation. For a beginner, I would suggest having a square hole drilled on the bottom of the beehive. This is to allow the bees to enter the beehive safely without encountering any obstruction while pollinating or for the honey extraction process. Once the holes are drilled, get brand new coverings and hives for the bees.

If you wish to have a successful beehive business, try to get a starter package from local apiary owners. If you have already acquired some of the tools and equipment from local hardware stores or the hobby shop, you might consider buying additional stuff to help you start with your beekeeping business. You may also consider selling beekeeping supplies through local shops or via online shops. You can even offer advice or suggestions for other beekeepers in your area or the community in general regarding how to deal with the honey production and selling beeswax. Once the honey production is established, you can then expand your beekeeping operation and sell the honey for higher prices.

For first time beekeepers, it is best to invest in a starter package of beehives. Some beekeepers make more money through renting out their hives once they become experienced enough. They make an average of $200 profit from renting out a single hive every three months. However, this depends on how many hives the beekeeper has and how far apart the hives are spaced.

A beginner beekeeper needs to purchase beehives and a starter set of frames from local hardware stores or apiary suppliers. After the purchase, the beekeeper needs to buy bee products for his or her hive. There are two kinds of bee products that a beekeeper needs: those used for the bees and the beeswax.

The most sold bee products are bee pollen, honey and beeswax. A good starter package will provide the beekeeper with a large variety of these bee products. This way, the beekeeper can choose among the most effective brands and also have a wide array of products to choose from.

Aside, from purchasing beehives, a good beekeeper should also purchase a smoker. A smoker is used to calm the honeybees down so that they can be transferred to a new location without being harmed. In order to minimize marketing costs, the smoker should only be used during nighttime. The beekeeper then moves on to the next part of the beekeeping process: marketing.

Marketing is basically telling people about your business. A good example of this is giving out flyers.

These flyers contain information such as the time frame of when you will be harvesting your honey bee hives and how much profit you will be making. Other marketing methods include putting up signs at malls and local coffee shops.

Aside from using flyers and signposts, another way to make money as a beekeeper is to buy feeds for your bees. These feeds will help the bees produce more bee larvae. The larvae will be used in making honey. Good feed supplements will usually contain royal jelly. Many beekeepers make use of honey as a source of income. It is highly recommended by experts because it is highly priced and can easily be obtained.

In order to sell their products or services, some beekeepers turn to agents who are known as "bee consultants" or "bee wholesalers." The success of a beekeeper is determined by the amount of work they put in and the time devoted to beekeeping. It's recommended for new beekeepers to secure a full-time contract to work in the field of beekeeping, starting with selling supplements.

It takes about thirty grams of honey to make one cup of royal jelly. You can also sell these honey cups through your local beekeeper association or online via eBay. You can make about $30 to $40 for each gram of honey sold.

Chapter 1
Choosing the Colony

Alright, you are good to go up, got the hives, got the suit, and got the super ultra-honey extractor 2000, what's the deal? It's called beekeeping for an explanation; you want bees to keep. This is the place where you would need to search out help the most.

Establishing your first beehive can be an intriguing experience, and there are a few tips that can apply to any type of set-up. There are two main methods of starting a colony: traditional gathering and artificial gathering. For beginners, I recommend the latter. It is much easier to purchase a fully equipped hive with all the necessary components such as core packs, pre-selected queens, and other items that simplify the process compared to traditional gathering.

Getting a multitude (normal amassing) requires a specific degree of abilities and smoothness to do it effectively, so I would recommend holding up to a minimum your subsequent season to endeavor regular amassing. Likewise, this strategy isn't something that you can prepare. Normal multitudes do happen, yet you can't really anticipate them as effectively.

Beginning new states is a spring interaction. You can do it fundamentally any time other than winter, however you want to do it in the late winter when you are sure that the colder time of year is finished. Bees need time to develop the brushes and stock honey and you need them to have however much time as could be expected to subside into the hive before you begin reaping honey.

One thing I might want to bring up is taking care of the "youthful" provinces. At the point when you start a province, and the year has not been too bright or the nectar stream season has been stopped for reasons unknown, ensure you leave sufficient honey in the hive for the colder time of year, and certainly feed the bees, regardless of whether you feel it's repetitive.

Presently, when you settle a state, keep an eye on it. The additional time you go through with your bees in the first place, the more stuff you will learn just by watching. Furthermore, trust me, beginning your first state will be an encounter that you will love for the remainder of your life. It resembles making your own little universe that adheres to specific guidelines and continues to compensate you in a wide range of ways.

The Most Common Bee Species

The most common bee species are:

Italian Bees

This kind of bee is the most popular race in the United States. First introduced in 1859, these bees replaced the original black or German bee brought by colonialists.

The Italian bee is usually brown or light yellowish and tends to have alternating stripes of black and brown on its abdomen. Those that have three abdominal bands, or five bands are known as leather-colored Italians and golden, respectively.

The Italian bee species usually starts brood-rearing in the spring and continues till late fall, which causes a large population during the entire active season. Also, most of the Italian bee strains are gentle and quiet on the combs. Since the Italian bees are usually many, they can quickly collect a considerable amount of nectar, which means more honey; however, they also require equally as much during winter.

The disadvantages of the Italian bees are that they have a weaker orientation than other races, which causes them to move from one colony to another, increasing their chances of contracting diseases.

However, they are considered great housekeepers, and the lighter color of the Italian queen makes it easier to spot her than is the case with other races. In addition, these bees are popular for producing great white capping that is useful for producing comb and honey.

Carnolians

This species usually has dark bees that are almost similar in appearance to the Caucasian except that they have brown spots or bands on their abdomen. Carolinas usually go through winter in small clusters and only start to increase rapidly when the first pollen becomes available in spring.

As a result, the major issue with this species is excessive swarming due to the rapidly increasing number of bees. The good thing is that during winter, the bees cluster in small numbers, making this species very economical regarding food consumption during winter.

They also don't move from one colony to another, which means they are well oriented and usually quiet on the honeycombs. They are usually available but are by no means common. Sometimes their stock is usually referred to as new World Carnolians and is considered the better version by some beekeepers.

Buckfast bees

The buck fast bee species is a hybrid product selected over a long time from a selection of many strains of bees from Southwestern England.

Studies have shown that the Buckfast bees are usually resistant to tracheal mites and are better suited for cool climates. Fortunately, these bees are easy to find because the US often imports Buckfast bee colonies.

Hybrid bees

The hybrid species is a combination of several lines or races of honeybees. Planned crosses result in a line of very prolific bees that portray something called hybrid vigor.

The best way to control hybrid vigor is mating. Commercial hybrids are usually a result of a combination of crisscrossing inbred lines developed and maintained for certain characteristics such as productivity, wintering, and gentleness.

Other Species

Aside from these well-known species, we have other species that have been developed for drug-resistant diseases as well as destructive parasites like mites.

Some of these species include the West Virginia selection, the buckeye strain from Ohio, and breeder queens from Buck fast Abbey in England. These bees have shown great results in terms of resisting tracheal mites. They have also been seen to have many other superior traits.

If you happen to use bees of a selected stock or hybrid bees in your hives, you will need to requeen regularly. Failing to replace the queen by allowing the natural process to take place tends to result to a loss of hybrid vigor; sometimes, it can make colonies to be difficult to manage – like being too aggressive/defensive.

Adult Bees

There are three different adult bees in a hive: the worker, drone, and the queen. Each plays a unique role within the colony.

1. The Queen Bee

The queen bee has a prominent abdomen. The abdomen is elongated and smooth and extends beyond her wings.

What role does the queen bee play?

The queen bee is more of a producer within the hive. It is important to note that the queen bee is the only reproductive female within the colony. She begins egg-laying in early spring. Egg-laying is initiated when the workers bring back the first fresh pollen. Production of eggs continue until fall. In some cases, eggs are produced continually if there is a constant supply of fresh pollen.

At the peak of her productivity, the queen bee can produce up to 2000 eggs daily. She has a life span of 5 years but may be productive for only 2-3 of these years. Younger queens produce plenty of eggs while the older ones produce plenty of drones. It is a common practice among beekeepers to requeen their hives once in a year or two. In most cases, the workers will replace the older queens without the knowledge or assistance of the beekeeper. An experienced keeper can groom queens of very high quality, but as a beginner, it is best that you buy an already-groomed queen from a good producer.

The Queen's Substance

Queen bees produce something known as queen substance. It is a pheromone. This pheromone or queen substance is a mixture of chemicals that is shared among all the bees in the hive just at the time when they're sharing food. If the queen disappears from the colony, her absence will be noticed within a couple of hours. Why? Because the worker bees will notice a significant drop in the level of pheromone. Faced with this situation, the workers move on to groom a new queen which is selected from the youngest larvae (1-3 days old). Also, the pheromones inhibit the development of ovaries in the workers. If the queenless period persists, some workers may begin laying. It is important to note that worker bees evaluate their queen based on the quality of pheromone produced by her. If the daily dose of pheromones received by the workers becomes insufficient, they will perceive her to be.

of poor quality. Preparations are then made to supersede here. It is easy to identify the queen. Most beekeepers mark her thorax with paint (usually a dot). This makes it easy to find her, and know if she's been replaced or not.

2. The Worker Bee

Worker bees are the smallest bees in the colony. They are also the most numerous. Worker bees are generally female and are incapable of reproduction. They also cannot mate but may lay unfertilized eggs when the colony gets hopelessly queen-less. The unfertilized eggs laid by the worker bees usually develop into drones.

As the name implies, workers perform all the tasks within a colony. These include:

- Secreting wax used for hive building or formation of honeycombs.
- They forage for pollen and nectar and produce honey from the nectar.
- They produce the royal jelly which is used to feed the young larvae and the queen.
- They tend to the queen and the larvae.
- They defend the hive and maintain optimal ventilating, heating, and cooling conditions.

Their eyes are well-developed. On the sides of their heads are their compound eyes, while three simple eyes lie at the vertex. They also have an elongated and well-developed tongue for extracting nectar from flowers.

Lifespan Of the Worker Bee

Workers have a life span of five to six weeks, i.e., workers groomed in the spring and early summer. They spend the first two weeks of their lives as house bees, working within the hive. The remaining three to four weeks is spent in the field, foraging for food. Workers that mature in the late fall may live healthily into the following spring. During the winter, worker bees cluster around the queen bee to keep her warm. When the queen resumes laying eggs, the worker bees must work hard to raise the first generation of bees the following year.

3. The Drones

Drones are basically male honeybees. They have just one role to play – and that is, fertilizing the young queen bee. The following are some of the major characteristics of drones:

- They are stouter and larger than the workers
- Their mouths are reduced
- Their eyes are large and distinctive, and meet on the top of their heads. The antennae of drones are slightly longer compared to those of the queen or the workers.

- Drones do not produce wax, tend the brood, or forage for nectar or pollen. They feed from the honey cells within the hive, or they may resort to begging from the workers.

- Drones are reared in the summer or spring. Rearing starts at least a month (4 weeks) before the queens are produced. With this, there will be more than enough healthy drones to mate with the queen.

- Drones spend their days eating and resting. They also patrol mating sites referred to as drone congestion areas.

During late summer, food quantity declines, and so does drone production. Drones are usually chased from the hives by workers just before the winter. A queenless colony may develop laying workers. Of course, these workers can only produce drones. If this happens, then such colony is lost forever. Their last attempt at maintaining the colony's genetic line will be to produce many drones who will then attempt to mate with a virgin queen from another colony.

Swarms

Bee swarming contributes to the development of the bee colony. When bees swarm, they do so because the hive is overcrowded. To create a swarm, an old honeybee queen will fly out of the hive with half of the worker bees, leaving behind a new queen with the other half of the workers. Bees in the

wild swarm most in early summer or late spring. Swarming is usually done at humid times of the day. All healthy bees swarm. In fact, it is part of their life cycle, but bee colonies often place restrictions on the incidence of swarming in domesticated bees.

A swarm may contain hundreds if not thousands of worker bees, plus a queen. The flight is temporary, after which they cluster and rest on tree branches and shrubs. They may rest for a couple of hours to a few days before resuming their flight. The rest period depends on the weather conditions and the amount of time required to search for a new hive site. When a new location is discovered, the cluster flies at once to the new site.

It is important to note that swarms do not harm anyone. Swarming bees have no nest to defend nor young ones. This reduces the tendency to sting.

But on the other hand, a swarm may sting when provoked. Why? Because the workers will attempt to safeguard their queen. If you find a swarm near your garden or home, simply call a pest control expert. They will help you relocate or exterminate the swarm. Remember that honeybees may be a protected species in some parts of the world, so it is important that you check with an expert before taking any action.

HOW TO Get Bees

When it comes to bees, bees again are sold by the pound with one queen. They're either sold as two pound or three-pound packages. I start looking for commercial packages that are available for sale in late December and early January. Why do I start in December/January? Well, the commercial producers of bees, who are in the business of selling packages of bees need to know how many they have to produce, or a target number. So, it is best that you order in December or January.

As a beginner, you should buy two packages, and buy or make two hives. You may also want to buy three-pound packages. That extra one pound of bees of worker bees, will enable you to have a little bit of honey production in your first year. That extra one pound of bees enables your hive to go through the summer, into the fall and through the winter as strong as it can possibly be. when you keep two hives, you'll have the opportunity to compare both hives. If you notice that one of your hives are weak, you can supplement or augment the weak hive from the strong one. So, it is best that you purchase or make two hives and two packages of bees. And with that, you can kickstart a lifelong hobby for you and your family.

Connecting with your local beekeeping association is the ideal place to start. This comes highly advised. Connect and converse with as many knowledgeable beekeepers in your area as you can. They will be able to provide you valuable advice on where to buy bees that will thrive in your region.

The adaptability of honeybees is one of their unique traits, allowing them to thrive in a variety of temperatures. For this reason, I prefer to collect feral swarms for my beekeeping endeavors. Unlike herds of cows or packs of dogs, swarms have a different way of reproducing naturally. When the queen and half of the worker bees leave the hive, it is known as a swarm. The remaining bees will raise new queens while scout bees search for a suitable location to form a new hive. These swarms can then be captured and used to populate an empty hive

What are the advantages of using swarms to fill your hive?

They first flourish in your region's climate. Since they are native to the region where they were discovered, these bees are virtually always certain to have survived the winter there. They get a thumbs up since they were capable of splitting in the early spring, are ready to begin growing comb right away, and can be incorporated into any high style.

Swarms are now used to populate hives, aiding in the local honeybee industry's goal of strengthening genetic diversity. Although the word "swarms" may sound somewhat frightening, honeybees are actually the calmest at this time. Before leaving the hive, they consume all the honey they can carry because they have no honey or offspring to guard. While searching for a new home, full bees find it challenging to sing and are instead preoccupied with their current predicament.

Swarms can be captured or lured into traps using bait. By early spring, set your traps and register with your local swarm list. Early March through late June are the times when swarms are most active in the Pacific Northwest. Thorns may appear later in the season, but they are typically small, don't have much time left in the growing season to establish a new colony, and don't produce enough honey reserves to last through the winter. It's not a certainty that a swarm will populate your hive because swarm capture is a growingly popular activity in beekeeping.

Are you planning to start your hive this year? When the season begins, you might want to obtain a source of bees. One of the few ways to make sure you have access to bees that can potentially populate any type of hive is to reserve a honeybee package.

Select The Most Appropriate Plants for your Honeybees

Consider the following before selecting a plant:

- Is it an excellent source of food for bees?

- When does it begin to bloom?

- Is this a native species?

Excellent Source of Food for Bees

You want to select plants that have a high nectar and pollen content. Avoid hybridized plants; many lack pollen and nectar, rendering them useless to your bees. Most wildflowers are quite high in nectar and pollen.

What many of us consider weeds, bees regard as an excellent food source. Dandelions and white clover are excellent sources of nectar for bees. Therefore, reconsider eliminating that "weed" from your grass.

Blooming Cycle.

You want to select a range of plants that bloom throughout the year to guarantee that your bees have abundant food to eat and store for the winter. When selecting plants for your bees, plant some in the spring, some in the early summer, and others in the late summer.

Indigenous Plants.

While many claim that native plants are the greatest for native bees, any plant containing nectar and pollen will attract bees and provide a nice diversity of food. It is best to supply a diverse array of plants.

Even if you choose the most beautiful plant for your bees, they appreciate variety. Consider this: Would you want to eat steak every day? Bees are similar; they want diversity not just for taste but also for health. Different flowers have unique characteristics that aid bees in maintaining a healthy immune system.

Borage - this plant produces copious amounts of honey in the spring.

Sunflowers come in a wide variety of kinds and are found practically everywhere. Honeybees simply adore them!

Tansy- This flower produces nectar and pollen for our bee friends and blooms for two months in the spring.

White clover is an excellent plant for providing nectar and honey to your bees in the spring.

Rhododendron- grows naturally in late spring in Washington and Oregon. Also, the lovely plants provide an abundance of food for your bees.

Goldenrod blooms from mid-summer to fall, providing an additional food source for bees.

Echium- blooms throughout the summer and provides bees with honey and pollen.

Lavender is a beautiful herb and provides an excellent food supply for bees in the late summer.

Cornflower - is a stunning wild blue flower that attracts bees in the late summer.

Chapter 2
Starting the Colony

Now that you have perceived the science of bumble bees, you can begin raising your own honey bee settlement so you can deliver honey. This section will talk about the basics of beginning your own bumble bee colony.

Where To Get Honeybees

When in doubt, it is crucial for begin raising bumble bees during spring. There are a few choices where you can get bumble bees to begin your beekeeping side interests. The following are your choices on the most proficient method to get your bees.

Swarm Or Feral Bees

Ask a nearby beekeeper in your place to get a multitude of wild honeybees. The justification for why wild honeybees are extraordinary is that they will generally endure better since they could have come from a state that is sufficiently able to endure the components. Getting swarm honeybees is a decent choice since they are fit to the nearby environment. You can set up lure and traps to get swarm honeybees zooming around your area.

Beekeeping Packages

You can get honeybees by purchasing from a raiser. The honeybee bundle contains ne sovereign with 10,000 honeybees from various states. Every one of the honeybees are set in a case that contains sugar syrup which will fill in as the food of the honeybees during transport. This is particularly evident assuming the honeybees will come from another state and should be conveyed through USPS.

Nucleus Colonies

Nucleus is a laid-out province that is held inside a five casing box. The best thing about core settlements is that you can move them to greater casing boxes so their populace can extend faster.

Equipment For Beekeeping

To become a successful beekeeper, it is essential to invest in proper beekeeping equipment. Not only will it help you manage your hives effectively, but it will also protect you while handling honeybees. This section will discuss the necessary gear required to start beekeeping. Hive tool: The hive tool is the most important equipment for any beekeeper. It allows you to inspect your hives and add new boxes as needed. Bees use propolis to seal their hives, so the hive tool is necessary for opening and examining the colonies.

Smoker: A smoker is one more fundamental piece of gear utilized in beekeeping. Honeybees are normally forceful bugs however in the event that you present smoke in the state, it will repress them by making it hard for them to communicate.

Bee brush: The honeybee brush is utilized to tenderly eliminate the honeybees off the brush or move them to somewhere else where you need them to be. Utilize the honey bee brush appropriately so you don't wind up harming your bees.

Personal defensive gear: The individual defensive hardware that beekeepers should utilize incorporates gloves and a coat with cloak to safeguard yourself from being stung in any case. Notwithstanding, when you become acclimated to working with bumble bees, you can gradually work without gloves or the coat totally, yet this is profoundly deterred as honey bee sting can be dangerous.

Box shaper: A container shaper is a convenient instrument utilized by beekeepers. It isn't unexpected utilized in dividing open the feeders and slicing materials to construct the hives.

Duct tapes: There are incalculable of employments for conduit tape in beekeeping so make certain to keep them in handy.

Butterfly net: A butterfly net can be utilized to get honeybees that have gotten inside the house. You can likewise utilize it to get different bugs that shouldn't go close to your hives. For example, you can utilize it to get yellow coats that might attack the hives. You can likewise thump down spider webs that might trap your bees.

Bee Diseases

Bees are strong bugs, yet they can likewise be impacted with various sicknesses. You should safeguard your honeybees so you can keep a sound populace. On the off chance that your honeybees are caused by illnesses, it can without much of a stretch crash your honeybee populace and it very well might be hard for you to bring back a sound populace of honey bees. The following are the various kinds of honey bee illnesses that you should be attentive of.

Varroa Mites

Varroa vermin assault hatchlings and grown-up honey bees. They suck the blood of honeybees in this way debilitating as well as shortening their life expectancy. Varroa parasites are minuscule, yet you can determine whether your honeybees are plagued by the bugs is to search for missing legs or wings because of the disfigured winged infection which is conveyed by the bugs. The Varroa bugs favor the robot brood so you should examine the brood to eliminate the vermin. Assuming you have a vermin issue, you can execute controls in the brood by drone brood penance, powdered sugar tidying, scaling back of brood cell size, and establishment of base boards.

You can likewise utilize sanitizers however ensure that you don't make a difference it during honey gather since the honey might become unsuitable for consumption.

Acarine Mites

Acarine bugs are parasitic bugs that typically pervade the aviation routes of honeybees. When the tracheal vermin have stopped on to the aviation route of honeybees, it gradually makes it challenging for honeybees to inhale in this way they ultimately pass on. Acarine bugs are controlled with oil patties which arc produced using vegetable shortening blended in with powdered sugar. Whenever honey bees eat the glue, they get the shortening which disturbs the capacity of the vermin to recognize youthful honey bees so they stay in the first host until they pass on alongside it.

Small Hive Beetle

The little hive scarab, Aethina tumida, is a little insect that lives inside the hives. The creepy crawlies are not related to any infections, yet it can become overpopulated in the hive that it can drive honey bee states out. To dispense with the hive scarabs, you can involve pesticides explicit for little hive creepy crawlies. You can apply the pesticide inside the layers of the hive so the insects can get presented to the pesticides when they get inside the hive.

Wax Moth

Wax moths, Galleria mellonella, don 't assault honey bees however they feed on wax that honey bees used to make the honeycomb. To annihilate the wax moths, you can freeze the hive (without the honey bees) since wax moths can't make due in cold winter.

American Foulbrood

American foulbrood is brought about by the microorganisms Paenibacillus hatchlings. The hatchlings are tainted by the microbes through ingestion from food. The spores grow inside the stomach which rivals the sustenance of the hatchlings. If the hatchlings are not very much fed, they in the end vanish of malnutrition.

Chalkbrood

Chalkbrood is a sort of contagious sickness that contaminates the stomach of the hatchlings. The parasite contend the hatchlings for food subsequently making it starve and ultimately bite the dust. This contagious illness is normally apparent during spring. Hives contaminated with chalkbrood can be treated by expanding the ventilation of the hive.

Chronic Bee Paralysis Virus

Bees tainted with the persistent honey bee loss of motion infection regularly display unusual shuddering. They additionally can't fly along these lines they regularly creep on the ground. The infection normally influences a huge populace of honey bees so search for a bunch of honey bees that group along with swelled midsections. The swelled midsections are a sign of expanded honey sacs.

Dysentery

Dysentery is normal in an unfortunate hive. It emerges because of extensive stretches of the powerlessness to make purifying flights. This is particularly obvious throughout the colder time of year when honey bees can't push their losses outside the hive. What happens is that the stomach of honey bees gets engorged with dung that must be voided assuming honey bees take on flight. You can deal with your hive by eliminating all honey and supplanting it with sugar water or fructose which doesn't have toxic matter hence honey bees don't deliver as much defecation that will make their stomach become more bloated.

Colony Collapse Disorder

The state breakdown jumble is quite possibly the most inadequately perceived peculiarity saw among working drones. It was initially found in Florida, yet it has spread to all over North America as well as Europe. Unfortunately, there is no known treatment for the state breakdown disorder.

.

Chapter 3
Everything You Need To Know About Honey

oney is a sweet, viscous food substance that bees and other insects produce. Bees produce honey from the sugary secretions of plants (floral nectar) or from secretions of other insects (such as honeydew), by regurgitation, enzymatic activity, and water evaporation. Bees store honey in wax structures called honeycombs. The variety of honey produced by honey bees (the genus Apis) is the best-known due to its worldwide commercial production and human consumption. Honey is collected from wild bee colonies or from hives of domesticated bees, a practice known as beekeeping or apiculture."

Honey has been collected, used and exchanged by humans since at least the Bronze Age. It is the only food that delivers a set of substances for human metabolic needs that cannot be obtained from any other single source.

The use of honey is mentioned in early writings, including ancient Egyptian, Chinese, and Indian texts. It was a sweetener from early times and was used to sweeten cakes in Ancient Greece by 500 BC.

Harvesting Honey

Once the bees have done their work of storing up the honey, it is now up to you to harvest the honey.

How To Get The Honeycomb

Select the correct time for harvesting

From around 9 in the morning to 4 in the afternoon on a sunshiny day, most of the bees are usually out to forage. Since there will be essentially fewer bees to handle, ensure that you harvest your honey within this window.

The quality and yield of honey is also going to be affected by the season you decide to do the harvesting. The bees halt the production of honey during early fall and late summer to provide nourishment for their queen. Thus, the majority of the clusters will be empty. Due to this, the harvesting of honey should virtually take place a bit early in the season.

Harvest the honey at around 2-3 weeks following the prime flow of nectar.

Since you probably don't know how to tell when this happens, you may enquire the information from advanced local beekeepers, or you can weigh the hive each night for the entire midsummer to determine for yourself. When the hive gets bulkier as can be, it means that prime nectar flow is occurring, and it is almost time to do the harvesting.

Wear protective gear

When taking the honeycomb out of the hive, there's no sure way of preventing the bees from charging at you. Therefore, whenever you plan on harvesting honey, it's recommended that you wear a complete beekeeper's outfit. At the very least, ensure that you have bee-proof overalls, a veiled hat, and thick elbow-length gloves. Also, you should wear long pants and a long-sleeved shirt. If you will be beekeeping in the long term, it's better to try investing in a professional suit for beekeeping.

Smoke the bees away gently

After lighting up the smoker, begin moving behind the hive. Fill the entryway to the hive with smoke. Remove the lid carefully, then spread the smoke inside the opening. When you do this, it makes the bees move nearer to the hive, leaving you to the honeycombs which are close to the top.

Typically, a smoker may simply be defined as a can stuffed with newspaper. The newspaper is lit to facilitate the production of smoke then the smoke is pumped via the hose. When the smoke gets inside the colony, the bees respond as if their hive is up in flames; therefore, they load up on honey before getting drowsy and sinking down below the hive. This way, they won't be putting up much of a fight, if any at all.

Ensure that you use the minimal amount of smoke possible

You may alter the taste of your honey when you use too much smoke. Therefore, if you continue filling the colony with more smoke after a majority of the bees are settling below the hive, you'll just be ruining the taste of your final product.

Uncover the top

Remove the inner cover from the hive's top using a hive tool – like to a smaller crowbar. To lift the cover, just slide the hive tool below the cover, then press down on it.

Since bees produce a resin substance called "propolis" to seal off the hive's edges, you will need to use a specialized too to lift off the inner cover – the seal is surprisingly quite strong.

Blow off the bees

You might still find a couple of bees over the frame you intend to take out. Using a small electric or gas blower, you may do away with those bees safely. If a blower is not readily available to you, you may try using a specialized "bee brush" to virtually brush off the bees from the frame. However, it may be perilous to use bee brushes as they have a tendency of agitating the bees and making them more probable of attacking you and whoever is close enough. If you have any bees falling and getting stuck inside the honey before you get a chance of blowing them away, you will have to handpick them out.

Uncover your honeycomb

Bees produce beeswax to cap the honeycomb onto the frame. Remove the wax using a dull butter knife, fork, or uncapping knife until the honeycomb has been uncapped from either side of your frame.

If you happen to have extra frames in your possession, you can take out the whole frame to do the uncapping of the honeycomb away from the hive. Once you have removed the honey-filled frames, slide in the spare frames. This is typically advised as it helps in minimizing your general exposure to bees.

Transfer the honeycomb to a room that is enclosed

Leaving the honeycomb out in the open is going to attract neighborhood bees. The scent of the honey will start the gathering of neighborhood bees on your yard in swarms where they will "rob" (feed sumptuously on your honey) which makes the harvesting process less successful and harder. Thus, immediately you take the honeycomb out of the hive, go process it since the honey is somewhat in a fluid state at this point. When you let it rest, it may begin to harden.

*If by chance your honey hardens before processing, simply allow it to rest in a sunny warm place for a couple of minutes to get it to gently warm up and make the honey fluid again.

You can harvest the honey using various methods. These include:

Method 1: Using An Extractor To Harvest Honey

Slide the frame into the extractor

Irrespective of the model you use – hand cranked or electric - you'll be required to insert the honeycomb frame (s) inside the machine's barrel then clip or snap them in position.

The specific method you will require following when you secure the frames inside the machine is going to differ from one model to another. Ensure that you perceive how your model works if you don't have the user's manual.

Rotate the frames

Switch on the machine and allow the motor to do its job or crank it up by hand. The honey is going to be forced to the barrel's wall as the frames are spun by the extractor. From there on, it will be flowing down to the bottom.

Use cheesecloth for straining the honey

Position a few pieces of cheesecloth over the top of your collecting bucket, then transfer the covered bucket below the spigot beneath your extractor. Turn on the spigot to allow the honey to flow through the cheesecloth.

When you strain the honey, it helps to get rid of bits of wax, honeycomb or any other debris that might have gotten into the honey while you were extracting the frame. You will have to be quite patient as the straining and extraction process may take a couple of hours.

Also, it is good to note that some people prefer to see some particles inside the honey jars as they think this signifies that the honey is of top 'raw' quality. Thus, it would be good to know your buyers if you are planning to sell the honey.

Method 2: Harvesting Honey With No Extractor

Transfer the honeycomb to a huge bucket

Remove the honeycomb from the frame if you haven't done so yet. Separate the honeycomb into enough pieces to fit the bucket well. You may use your hands for this part to disintegrate the honeycomb.

Press the honeycomb using a big masher until it becomes a thick mush.

Once you are done, the honeycomb is supposed to be really crushed such that you won't be able to remove any of the bits using your bare hands.

Straining your honey

Place a couple of cheesecloth layers, nylon straining bag, or strainer over the collecting bucket. Gradually strain the crushed honeycomb through your available straining technique allowing the honey and debris to separate – where the honey will strain into the collecting bucket and the debris will be left on the strainer. Again, you will need to exercise more patience as this stage might take up a couple of hours to finish.

You may attempt to speed up the process by crushing a honeycomb that has already been crushed in your hands over a strainer. This process may be super messy and is still going to take quite some time to complete. At times, there's a bit of the crushed honeycomb that's left behind the bucket. In this case, you'll need to use a scraper to scrape the bottom and sides of the container.

How To Package The Honey

• Clean your containers thoroughly. Use hot soapy water to wash the bottles or jars you intend to use.

• Rinse properly, then dry fully.

• Use plastic or glass containers.

• Ensure that you clean the containers entirely regardless of whether they are new or not to prevent honey contamination.

• Bottle your honey up. Position a funnel over the jars, then pour the honey into the freshly cleaned containers or simply spoon it into the jars. Secure the bottles or jars using airtight lids.

• For the first couple of days after packaging the honey, you will need to keep an eye on the jars. If there was any debris remaining in the honey, after 2-3 days, all of it should deposit on the surface of every jar. Discard the debris before sealing off the honey-filled container for storage in the long term.

Store the honey and then enjoy as you please.

So long as you seal the container well, it's possible to store natural organic honey at room temperature for several months. The honey you yield from the harvest is going to vary depending on the health of the bees, size of honeycomb, time of season you do the harvesting, and the general success of the entire season. In suitable conditions, **a single honeycomb may yield approximately 1.6kgs (3 ½ lbs) of honey.**

Beekeepers typically do the harvesting of the honey at the end of a relevant nectar flow, and the hive is full of capped honey that is cured. Circumstances and conditions are utterly distinct throughout the entire country.

For the first time beekeepers, you'll be lucky to yield a small amount of honey during the first year near the end of summer. This is because a new colony will require an entire season to put together a population that's adequately extensive to collect abundant honey.

During summer, it is recommended to check inside the colony after every few weeks. Take note of the sort of progress the bees make, then probe on the frames that are full of capped honey. You are free to take out a shallow frame and harvest it once it is 80% (and above) filled with capped honey that is sealed. Alternatively, you may try being patient and leave the frames in the hive until one of the following things occurs:

- The final prominent nectar flow of the season is finished

- All frames are full of capped honey

You may extract honey from open cells as long as it's cured. To know whether it is cured, simply turn the frames upside down to have the cells face the earth. Gently shake the frame. If the liquid flows from the cells, stop the extraction as it's not cured. It's not honey at all; just nectar that has not undergone curing. It has a really high-water content to be regarded as honey. When you try to package the nectar in bottles or jars, you'll get the resulting water-like syrup, which will probably ferment and go bad.

Again, you will need to be patient and give the bees the time they require to collect as much honey as they can. It's normal for things to get a bit busy during the season; just ensure that you do all the essential tasks. But then you shouldn't allow your honey supers to remain in the hive for a long time; otherwise, you may end up with either of the following unpleasant situations:

- The bees will start to consume the honey that they have produced following looms of winter across the far horizon and the final prime nectar flow. When you are late for harvesting, the bees are going to consume most of the honey you were hoping to harvest.

- Alternatively, they may begin to transfer the honey deeper in the hive into open cells. Regardless of what happens, you'll lose honey that was supposed to be for you, so make sure that you extract the honeycombs before it occurs.

- When you take a long time to harvest, the weather becomes cold, causing the honey to thicken up (or worse, granulation), making it impossible to extract the honey. Keep in mind that the simplest way of harvesting honey is while it flows easily in the summer warmth.

All these situations can be avoided if you remain vigilant while observing the nectar flow. After all, you are putting in the work to be able to consume the honey once the process is completed.

But something else that can quickly deprive you of honey is having a hive that has lost its queen. Let's explore this topic next.

Chapter 4
The Evolution of The Colony

Honey bees are very social insects, and as a result, they live together in groups called colonies and have their dependence on each other for their survival. In a colony, most of the bees there are sterile females and are called worker bees. The male ones are called drones, and their only work in the colony is to mate with the queen. Most of the time, there is just one queen bee, the fertile female, and her work is to maintain or improve the colony's population by laying more eggs.

Worker bees could be within the range of 1,000 to 60,000, depending on the ability of the queen bee to lay eggs, the available space to expand the hive, and the amount of food that comes in for the colony. The lifespan of worker bees is about six weeks. Their job includes getting food and water for the entire colony, doing all the housework, and protecting the hive against any invasion or intrusion. They are also in charge of cooling the hive and maintaining the temperature and humidity of the hive at a constant, regardless of whatever the conditions outside are. If the colony loses its queen, the worker bees may also have to lay eggs, but the eggs they lay will not help improve the colony's population because the worker bees can only lay drones.

The amount of drones in a bee colony fluctuates depending on the season. During the winter, there may be none at all, but during the summer, you can spot several. As the fall season arrives and food sources become scarce, worker bees force out the drones from the hive.

When she is about a week old, the queen bee starts flying out of the hive to mate in the air with one or more drones. After she returns to the hive, she starts laying eggs. In her lifetime, she lays thousands of eggs, which means that she could lay as much as 1000 eggs per day. Each egg is put in a separate cell of the honeycomb. On the third day after the laying of the egg, it becomes a larva. The worker bees, which also play the role of nursemaids, start to feed, nurture, and take care of the larva until it becomes a pupa. The workers then seal the pupa into its honeycomb cell so that it can complete its development. On the twenty-first day after the laying of the egg, an adult bee comes out.

Bee Strains

The most common strain of bees in the United States is the Italian strain. These bees are very hardworking and very gentle too. The Caucasian strain is another strain that is also common. These bees are gentler than the Italian bees, but their queens are very dark and hard to find when there is a cluster of bees. It is something to note. After all, you must be able to locate your queen bee because you may have to replace her after a year or so if she reduces the number of eggs she lays and cannot maintain the colony's population.

Caucasian bees make use of an outrageous amount of a gummy substance called propolis in their hives. They take this substance from buds and trees that are injured. It is a sort of cement in their hives. As a result, if a frame is heavily propolyzed, it becomes very difficult to remove that frame.

There are available hybrid bees, bees that are usually a cross between two or more bee strains. These bees are usually more productive than regular bees. The major issue they have is that their offspring will have no resemblance to the original hybrid bees you had after about a year or two. If you make up your mind to use hybrid bees, it is usually advisable to replace your queen every year. This replacement will help to give you a uniformly strong colony.

Colony feeding

There are times of the year when food supplementation is necessary; this happens twice a year:

In spring: stimulatory feeding. This is done using artificial syrups composed of water and sugar, which act as substitutes for nectar.

In autumn-winter: overwintering. During the winter, there is a stop of colony activity, and there is no flowering. This overwintering is provided when there are not enough food reserves to survive until the following spring. Feeding is done using mash or candy, which are substitutes for pollen.

Feeders provide artificial feeding in the form of racks or three-kg bags.

There are various formulations of syrup, among which are:

- Sugar (40%) + water (60%). To increase the queen's posture
- Sugar (50%) + water (50%). To maintain the population.
- Chancaca (half cap in the hive). To maintain the population.
- Chancaca (one bundle per 4.5 liters of water) to stimulate laying.
- Honey (50%) + water (50%). It is the mixture most used by beekeepers

It is the mixture most used by beekeepers for maintenance or stimulation of laying.

Beekeeping Safety

For those new to the beekeeping industry, there are likely a lot of aspirations in mind, such as distinguishing between queens and worker bees, familiarizing oneself with eggs and brood, determining optimal hive locations, and absorbing all possible information about these buzzing insects.

Another important target that you should keep in mind is your own protection during bee inspection. Although beekeeping is quite an interesting venture, it is important to note that it is not without risk.

You'll be living in close quarters with tens of thousands of stinging insects that hate disruptions and will valiantly protect their home if they consider you as a threat. It's a good idea to do your research about safety tricks and treat your passion with care. Here are a few tips to keep you safe when working in the apiary.

Do your work carefully

Bees do not like surprises, such as disturbance in their happy home. So, you will continue to make the routine "checkup" or make it easy for the bees by working carefully. Have you ever seen how tapping on a hive produces a brief burst of rapid buzzing? Since bees hate noisy sounds, always try to keep the sound as low as possible, with little bumps and bangs.

You'll have a better time with fewer bees taking flight around you if you can give the "risk" warning (your smoker plays a key role in this). Take your time, but don't leave your hives open for a longer period of time. Work consciously, keeping in mind all the risks.

Inspect during pleasant weather

Always select a warm, sunny afternoon if you're going to do simple routine work in your hives, such as tracking eggs and brood or testing the honey and pollen. The main reason behind this is, on a sunny day, your hive will have fewer bees inside, so more of the workers will be out "working."

So it will be easier and safer to work in this less-crowded hive because you'll be less likely to disturb the bees. Furthermore, some beekeepers claim that a colony is usually "angrier" on rainy or stormy days, so they don't work in the hive on a rainy day.

Wear proper protective cloths

Many beekeepers like to work without hats, in normal clothing, or even without a veil. Does it mean that they're not scared of being stung? Perhaps not at this stage. They've probably dealt with bees for so long that they can easily deal with them, and many experienced beekeepers appreciate the independence that comes with skipping gloves and other protective gear.

But this is not right. It's better to wear all protective clothing if you are a novice. Protective garments will give you peace of mind, helping you to focus more deeply on your job and learning about your bees' habits. It should also give you more confidence in going to work, particularly when bees start buzzing around your head and crawling up your hands.

Keep your Hive Tidy

It is also important to keep a clean environment around your hives. It will keep both you and your bees healthy, which can surprise you. Always empty your hive boxes, or make sure that old doors and comb should not be left standing, as this honey-scented stuff will lure skunks, raccoons, and even bears. These creatures are a danger to not only your hives but to you as well. Therefore, it is very important to keep things in proper order.

Maintain the cleanliness of your equipment

Your bees' wellbeing can be influenced by how you treat your hives and other supplies. You need to be very careful while using your equipment. A good cleaning can play an important role in avoiding the transmission of infection.

Be mindful that thorough cleaning and sterilizing of the hives and machinery can be very difficult. Before you begin, double-check that you have all the appropriate supplies and equipment for the job.

Have you ever wondered when do we disinfect our machines, supplies, and boxes?

When you carry your boxes for storage at the end of the season

- If the colonies are infected or diseased
- Every time you think about re-using one of your tools
- When you decide to transfer things from one colony to another.
- If the tools get old or infected with bacteria.

Lyme disease

Despite its many benefits, beekeeping comes with several possible threats and dangers. More recently, the high risk of contracting diseases like Lyme has become a major danger for beekeepers, especially in the northeastern United States.

Ticks can spread the bacteria that cause Lyme disease. As a result, beekeepers are strongly advised to search themselves for ticks when returning from the bee yard.

- Tick tests should be complete and conducted in a special setting.
- Tick-removal products are also available in the market to aid with tick removal.
- Wearing light-colored long-sleeved tops and long trousers to make ticks easier to find.

Without any doubt, beekeeping is all about learning more for the sake of your bees, the environment, and yourself. Experience, honey, and many other advantages that even you can imagine would be your reward. You will continue to enjoy your time in the hive as long as you are mindful of the issue that may arise and can take the necessary precautions to remain healthy.

Follow all these procedures and you can take the sting out of working with bees.

How to Maintain Queenright Colony

Every spring, it is recommended to replace the strongest queen in my hives to prevent overcrowding. A hive is less likely to swarm when the queen's pheromones are strong, and these pheromones are at their strongest during a first-year queen's reign. Many sources claim that a new queen is the most effective way to prevent swarming. However, it seems counterproductive to eliminate your best queens and replace them with untested ones. Plus, if the new queen is rejected, you are left with no queen at all.

Keep those sovereigns as opposed to executing them. To do this, eliminate the sovereign alongside an edge of brood and an edge of nectar and put them in a two-outline nuc. At that point, bring the new sovereign into the hive. If anything turns out badly with the new sovereign, you can generally once again introduce the former one, or on the other hand, you can keep her "for possible later use" for some other reason.

For instance, a new supply may give an impression of being queenless. The multitude constructed brush in which it put away possibly nectar, filter the honey bees through a sovereign excluder, If you'd did not see any queen, take one of your saved sovereigns and present her. When she begins laying the settlement will likely supplant her, however without her to kick things off, the entire multitude would pass on.

When I first started gathering sovereigns, I wondered what I would do when the two-frame nuclear units became too crowded. However, I discovered that these small settlements tend to expand until they fill the available space and then remain stable. In reality, they are not large enough to overcrowd or take over. So, they simply stay compact. In the past, I have kept these "reserve" sovereigns for the entire summer.

Here and there I just put a multitude of the cell, brood, and nectar in the little nucs. It appears to take everlastingly, however, the honey bees ultimately produce a laying sovereign and I simply leave her there. On the off chance that one doesn't succeed, I simply start another. Since I'm utilizing her just as reinforcement, it doesn't matter how long it requires.

Conclusion

Whether you have reached this point on purpose or because you have excess honey and wax, being a beekeeper can provide you with additional income. This section of the book discusses what you must consider if you want to earn a profit. It is time to advance in your pastime!

Prior to turning your pastime into a business, you must determine whether doing so is legal. Return to your research on your local zoning laws and homeowners association regulations to determine this. It might be as simple as a refresher to obtain this information, given that you may already be familiar with it through your research into the laws governing beekeeping. If you do not already have this information, use the contact you established previously to help you obtain it. Check local regulations regarding the sale of honey and wax to ensure they comply.

Plan your business model thoroughly before you begin selling; this involves determining operational costs, deciding where, what, and to whom you will sell, and determining operational costs. Operational expenses should not significantly exceed what you have already invested but be careful to account for any required business or operating permits. Consider whether you require additional insurance, as this could be a more financial burden than you imagine.

Consult the members of your club and professional beekeeping organizations for optimal preparation. They are likely the most up-to-date source of knowledge that will assist you in covering all bases. Many of them are likely also selling their items, so they will be familiar with the regulations, administrative obligations, and optimum locations for selling and advertising your products.

They will likely advise you not to immediately enter the commercial world. It is preferable to give yourself time to adjust to the responsibilities of a beekeeper before adding the additional pressure of attempting to make a profit.

Once you are confident in your talents as an apiarist and have created a business strategy, ensure that you have also thought out everything else. Depending on the quantity of honey you intend to sell, you may need to purchase a honey extractor if you do not already possess one. Depending on where you get it, the price might range between several hundred and several thousand dollars. However, the cost is definitely worth it, as you can extract more honey from the combs faster than with any other approach.

In addition to considering the honey, you must also determine how it will be packaged. Normal canning jars and lids can be used, but if you want to eliminate the wording and appearance of a standard jar, you should find a local source with additional possibilities. Avoiding raised letters is also beneficial for your labels, since they adhere more effectively to smooth surfaces. Check local laws about these labels; most states and provinces have strict regulations regarding what can and cannot appear on honey labels. As these are food goods, the applicable health and safety laws cannot be disregarded.

The final aspects of your business are to examine are the more enjoyable ones. What will you be selling? Honey is the most obvious option, but you can also offer beeswax alone or in combination with other products, as well as pollination services. This could be accomplished by renting the desired amount of hives to, say, a farmer. They would then pay you rental fees in addition to the labor and maintenance costs you would incur in the form of routine inspections. If you reside at a greater distance, you may consider charging for travel time.

If you have sufficient bees and want to expand your business, you can even consider selling the bees themselves. By isolating a few frames from the rest of the hive, you can create your own nuc colonies. Permit them to produce a new queen and give them the winter to grow strong. In the spring, the little colony will be available for sale.

There are numerous alternatives for what you could sell. Diversify your items to provide your company the greatest strength. Dependence on one or two products is likely to result in less profit than desired.

Determine who you will sell to and how you will do it after determining what you will be selling. Will you be selling at local farmer's markets? Count on word-of-mouth? Become a vendor at a local artisan store? Have a web-based store? There are countless options, so be careful to examine the benefits and drawbacks of each. The desire for fresh, locally produced goods has never been higher, so turning your hobby of beekeeping into additional income should be a breeze!

Book 4

Backyard Beekeeping guide

Introduction

The honeybee population tremendously benefits from the fascinating pastime of backyard beekeeping. As individuals strive to live and eat more sustainably, beekeeping is gaining popularity. Your backyard beehive brings your garden to life by pollinating your plants for optimal yield.

Bees are remarkable, small creatures tasked with pollinating the plants that provide us with avocados, cherries, melons, broccoli, and a myriad of other delicious foods. However, these critical pollinators are becoming extinct at an alarming rate. Honeybees are threatened by habitat loss, tracheal and varroa mite infestations that kill them in large numbers, and electromagnetic radiation from smartphones that impairs their navigational skills.

The honeybee population tremendously benefits from the fascinating pastime of backyard beekeeping. As individuals strive to live and eat more sustainably, beekeeping is gaining popularity. Your backyard beehive brings your garden to life by pollinating your plants for optimal yield. Your efforts are rewarded with an abundance of golden honey straight from the comb. This raw, unpasteurized honey is substantially more palatable and nutrient-dense than supermarket honey, which has been pasteurized and stripped of many of its vital components.

If you're considering starting a bee colony as a pastime to rescue the bees and enjoy locally produced honey, this article will provide an outline of what you'll need and how to get the most out of it.

Chapter 1
Backyard Beekeeping

If you've been thinking about starting a bee colony in your backyard, you may have thought about managing your colony. One of the most important things to consider is whether there is enough food for them. In most cases, this means honey! But what exactly is honey? How do you know if there are enough resources for your bees? And most importantly, how can you manage your hive to produce more honey than it consumes? I'm here to answer all these questions and more.

Understanding The Honey Flow

The honey flow is the time of year when nectar is available for bees to collect. This season occurs in the spring and summer, so beekeepers should be aware of what is happening with their bees at this time.

A beekeeper needs to know about the honey flow to plan what kind of activities they will be able to do during this period. If you are starting out, you may only want to harvest your honey once or twice a year, but if you have been keeping bees for some time, it might be worth considering taking full advantage of the season by harvesting more often than that.

What is the Honey Flow?

The honey flow is the time of year when bees collect nectar and make honey. The time it takes for a colony to fill its hives with honey depends on many factors, including the location and weather conditions, but it usually lasts from a few weeks to several months. The duration of the honey flow can vary greatly depending on where you live: for example, in some regions, it may last all summer long, while in others, there might not be any major flows at all!

The weather is one of the main influences on whether your bees will have enough resources (food) available during their critical period each year when they need to reproduce. Suppose there isn't enough pollen or nectar available. In that case, they won't be able to produce enough food stores to survive through wintertime until next spring when more new flowers arrive again after being dormant since the fall/winter season began last year...

When Does the Honey Flow Occur?

Many different factors affect when bees collect nectar, pollen, and water. The time of year is one factor. For example, nectar flows during the spring and summer, whereas pollen flows occur during the spring and fall.

The weather is another factor that affects when your bees will be out collecting nectar or pollen from plants in your backyard or elsewhere in the neighborhood. If it's hot outside and there's no rain forecasted for days, your bees may stay inside their hive to keep cool instead of going outside to collect food for themselves and their colony members (worker bees). If it has been raining lately but then gets hot again on a certain day of interest to you as a backyard beekeeper, this can also cause your honeybees' behavior patterns to change significantly as they try to figure out how best to respond both individually and collectively within their colony structure (hive).

How to Spot the Honey Flow

You can spot the honey flow by looking for a change in the weather, such as a shift in temperature or humidity. You may also notice bees flying around more than usual, so they're busy pulling nectar from flowers. If you see plants blooming and producing flowers, there's a good chance that they'll be covered with bees soon enough.

What Beekeepers Can Do to Help

If you're a backyard beekeeper, there are several things you can do to help your bees thrive. First, you'll need to manage the food sources available to them by keeping weeds and other plants that bloom in late spring or summer under control. Doing this will reduce competition with other pollinators who may move in on your territory and steal away resources that could otherwise go toward growing honey.

Secondly, by managing the weather through plantings and irrigation systems around the hive-site, beekeepers can make sure their bees have enough water throughout the year—even during hot summers when they may struggle without it!

Finally, if possible, through research into local climate conditions (e.g., whether there are any nearby wetlands where native plants grow) then having some knowledge about what kinds of flowers might benefit from these sites would be helpful too (I'm thinking especially about cattails but perhaps also rushes).

Proper planning and management of your foods can help you get the most out of your bee colony.

If you plan to do any backyard beekeeping, it's important that you understand the honey flow. A honey flow is a period of time in which many flowers bloom and bees have a high demand for nectar. The nectar collected during this time will be used to produce honey.

Proper planning during this period is essential to get the most out of your bee colony and ensure they're producing rich and tasty honey. It involves understanding when your area has its main flower sources, how much food your hive needs daily to survive through winter, what kind of weather conditions are best suited for collecting pollen (warm days with cool nights), and where they can find water sources that aren't contaminated by chemicals or pesticides (rivers/streams).

The honey flow can be a great way for beekeepers to make extra money, but it requires careful planning. It's important to know when the honey flow is happening in your area so you can plan accordingly and monitor your bees carefully. Proper management of your hive will ensure success!

How to Open the Hive

Direct smoke by the passage before the hive, to confound the watchman honey bees. Lift the external cover somewhat and direct a couple of puffs of smoke under it. Allow the cover to withdraw tenderly and sit tight for one to two minutes for the smoke to produce results.

Eliminate the Outer Cover

Eliminate the hive's external cover and deliberately put it on the ground. Direct some smoke into the opening in the inward cover, if you have one. Trust that the honey bees will respond to the smoke.

Eliminate the Inner Cover

Utilize your hive instrument to delicately pry up the internal cover and eliminate it. On the off chance that there is wax or propolis on the inward cover, utilize your hive instrument to scratch it off. Set the internal cover on top of the external cover on the ground, being mindful so as not to harm any honey bees.

Eliminate the Honey Super

Pry up the top box—the nectar super—utilizing your hive apparatus. Takeoff the super and set it on top of the inward cover. The nectar super can be a shallow, medium, or profound box.

On the off chance that the hive has a second nectar super, smoke and eliminate in this case as well. On the off chance that the hive has a sovereign excluder situated underneath the nectar supers, eliminate it with the hive device and put it in a safe spot.

Note: Young states may not yet need nectar super. On the off chance that yours doesn't have one, continue down to the profound boxes holding the state.

Smoke the Second Deep Box

Tenderly puff smoke into the following hive box. This is known as the subsequent profound, which in many hives is one of two boxes that hold the brood province. On the off chance that you have three medium boxes rather than two deeps, you'll simply rehash this twice until you get to the base box. You will begin your investigation with the base box.

Eliminate the Second Deep Box

Eliminate the subsequent profound and spot it tenderly on top of the nectar super or internal cover. You will review this container later.

Eliminate the First Frame

Start your assessment with the main (base) profound box. Direct smoke in the middle of the edges, at that point, eliminate the primary edge and set it either in a casing holder or tenderly on top of the other hive boxes or on the inward cover, taking consideration not to harm any honey bees.

How to Remove Bees from the Hive

Each cautiously pry each casing free utilizing your hive apparatus, at that point lift the casing and examine it:

Attempt to recognize the sovereign. This is simpler if she's checked, yet it's yet conceivable on the off chance that she isn't. Search for her long, thin, unstriped midsection and a circle of laborers around her. On the off chance that you can't discover the sovereign, it's critical to discover eggs, which demonstrate the sovereign was there in the previous one to three days.

Check for any parasites or irritations—bugs, wax moth hatchlings, foulbrood, and so on. Decide the number of edges is drawn out—loaded up with look over-prepared for nectar. At the point when seven of 10 edges are attracted to the base profound box, it's an ideal opportunity to add the subsequent profound box. At the point when seven of 10 are attracted the subsequent profound, add a nectar super. If the nectar super is near full, add another.

Check for Larvae

Part of examining the casings is searching for brood—covered and uncapped hatchlings and eggs. Appeared here is a lovely example of creating, uncapped hatchlings—this is the thing that you're searching for in your colony of bees review.

Search for Eggs

Distinguishing eggs is the main piece of the bee colony investigation for the new beekeeper, however, novices regularly discover the eggs hard to spot. Eggs look like meager grains of rice. There ought to be one for each cell, laid in the middle. On the off chance that you have more than one egg for each cell, your hive has laying working drones—counsels an accomplished beekeeper about the present circumstance.

The most ideal approach to see eggs is to hold the casing shifted up toward the sky at around a 30-degree point, with the brilliant sun sparkling behind you. Hold it marginally to the side of you with the goal that the shadow example of a cross-section from your shroud doesn't darken the eggs.

Utilizing understanding glasses or an amplifying glass can likewise help. You can shift the edge to and fro and try different things with the point of the sun and the edge until you see them. The base focus of the edge is generally the best spot to emphatically distinguish eggs.

Supplant the Frames

As you assess each casing, put it out from the dark space left by the past outline you eliminated. Push each edge facing the one before it as you supplant it—delicately, to try not to harm any honey bees. Utilizing a honey bee brush or smoke helps move the honey bees far removed, particularly at the edge ears, where they are probably going to get squeezed.

Assess the casings altogether, and don't change their request during an investigation. At the point when you get to the last edge, push the entire arrangement of edges together as one single unit, utilizing your hive apparatus to make space in the front for the main casing. As you supplant the primary casing, utilize your hive device to even up space on one or the other side of the first and last edges so the arrangement of edges is focused in the crate.

Supplant the Second Deep and Honey Super

With the main profound box investigated, continue to the subsequent profound box, examining the edges, and afterward restacking the crate onto the primary profound box. Supplant the sovereign excluder, if your hive has one, supplant the nectar super. To do this, position the case with the edge on the back edge of the hive, at that point gradually "destroy" it forward, moving gradually to try not to harm any honey bees. You can utilize the smoker or honey bee brush to delicately move the honey bees far removed.

Supplant the Inner Cover

Slide on the inward cover utilizing the tractor strategy: Start toward one side and gradually slide the cover across the container. Utilize the smoker or honey bee brush to move honey bees far removed, depending on the situation.

How to Uncap the Honey

The primary significant advance is to eliminate the wax covering from the brush. In business tasks, this might be finished with a programmed "uncapper" that can eliminate covers from more than 600 edges each hour. The innovation utilized in uncapping fluctuates broadly, from the programmed to the electric hand-held uncapper, and afterward to a plain blade utilized physically. This last choice includes additional time and exertion.

Despite the favored innovation, the wax covering should be taken out to get the nectar out of the brushes. Eliminating the flimsy layer of wax doesn't harm the dividers of the cells, thus the honey bees can reuse similar cells.

At times, beekeepers eliminate the nectar outlines before the honey bees cap the cells. Frequently the nectar has not yet aged, thus it has high water content. The beekeeper should then dehumidify the edges before removing the nectar.

How to Extract the Honey

Extricating the nectar implies eliminating it from the hive outlines. To do this, the uncapped edges are turned in a machine called an extractor. Radiating power draws the nectar out of the brushes and into a repository. For this cycle to function admirably, the nectar should be adequately warm to stream, as it's ideal to separate it at the earliest opportunity after the edges have been taken out from the hives, while they contain some warmth. Something else, the casings ought to be left in a warm room preceding extricating.

Extractors change in size and in the kind of innovation they use, yet the mechanical standards contrast practically nothing. The littlest extractors are two-outline manual sorts, while some others are totally robotized, and can hold 120 edges immediately and measure more than 600 edges each hour.

How to Filter & Bottle your Honey

Once the nectar is extracted from its casings, it goes through a series of channels. Some of these channels rely on pressure, while others simply use gravity. This process ensures that no unwanted substances, such as dead honey bees or wax, end up in the final product. Depending on the target market, the nectar may be packaged directly into small containers for retail sales or large drums for storage or exportation. In order to appeal to a wide range of consumers, nectar is packaged in various sizes and styles of containers. These can include glass jars, plastic tubs, and squeezable bottles. The packaging stage can involve automation in larger operations or manual labor, such as hand-capping a plastic bucket in smaller operations.

How to aim for Honey Quality Over Quantity

Reviewing depends on qualities, for example, dampness content, independence from unfamiliar matter, and flavor. Nectar is reviewed on a size of 1 to 3, with 1 being the best. Supermarkets for the most part sell grade 1, as lower grades are utilized in business food handling.

Nectar is likewise arranged by shading. Prepackaged nectar is delegated white, brilliant, golden, or dull. Shading is generally dictated by the sort of blossoms visited by the honey bees. All in all, light-shaded nectar is more gentler and sweeter, while hazier nectar has a more grounded taste. It's about close-to-home inclination!

Chapter 2
Caring For Bees

I know you were all enthusiastic about the liquid gold and perhaps even the possibility of making money from keeping one or two hives. However, protecting the species is beekeeping's top concern and primary focus. Learning about the diseases and pests that can harm them is necessary. Bees, unlike some other animals, typically let you know when something is wrong. If your bees have any health issues, I will explain what to check for and offer possible solutions during hive inspections.

The key to keeping your hive healthy is to observe it regularly and record everything in your beekeeping journal. You can spot any changes in your bees by keeping a daily eye on them. Then, by occasionally going over your beekeeping record, you may compare seasons from one year to the next or, if you have multiple hives, even compare hives.

Why Do Bees Get Sick?

The species of honeybees has endured for countless millennia. Despite their seeming fragility, they are incredibly durable. Despite our best efforts, honeybees are wild insects that are tenaciously motivated to survive. No one has ever succeeded in keeping bees alive without giving them access to nature.

However, over time, it appears that more exposure to poisons and chemicals had an impact on their immune system. Beekeepers are searching for alternate treatment options because the disease treatments they have been using for the past 30 years are no longer as effective.

While many of the causes of bee illnesses are wholly beyond human control, some can be avoided. Your bees could become ill for a variety of reasons, including:

- Being cooped up inside for an extended period of time
- Climate
- Exposure to hazardous substances
- Bacteria and virus exposure
- Overcrowding
- Too much moisture
- Insects and arachnids in the hive
- Starvation
- Too much room

Preventing Illness

As mentioned before, there are certain aspects of our environment that we simply cannot control. A prime example of this is when I lost two entire colonies due to the county's use of chemical sprays in an attempt to reduce mosquitoes in our neighborhood. However, there are also times when we can take action to prevent stress and illness among our bees. While some factors may not directly lead to their deaths, they can weaken their immune systems and make them more susceptible to diseases and pests.

By expanding your hive with more boxes or supers or by dividing your colony to provide room for expansion, you can avoid overcrowding.

A concern with having too much space is that it allows for the growth of pests and predators. A hive that is too large for bees to defend and protect is difficult for them to do. Imagine a huge Hollywood gala with numerous entryways and a single bouncer at the door. There is no way that one bouncer could keep all the riffraff out. The same logic holds true when there are too many bees and not enough bees in the hive. This occurs when novice beekeepers try to fill their hive with all the boxes at once.

When a hive separates from a swarm or, occasionally, after the winter when a sizable section of the colony dies, a hive may also have too much space. To avoid this, make sure to get rid of any unused boxes and wait to add a new box until the bees have completed building comb on 34 of the existing frames.

It's simple to stop the bees from starving. Water and honey, or bee nourishment, are essential for your bees to survive. Your bees might be starving even when you assume there is plenty of food available for them to forage. When conducting inspections, always keep fresh water on hand and make sure their food supply or honey reserves are stocked. Create some food storage so they can survive the winter as well.

Numerous factors, such as illness, a shortage of food, predators, a new habitat, and excessive human meddling, can stress bees. But a major cause of bee stress is a lack of food and the excessive foraging that results from that. For this reason, I suggest that you plant your bee garden before erecting your hives.

Signs of Sickness

The value of observation and keeping a beekeeping notebook cannot be overstated. Even anything as straightforward as "Bees are flying a lot today" might be noted. Trust me, you'll be glad you took thorough notes.

Observable signs that anything is wrong that you can see from outside the hive include:

Excessive amounts of dead bees: There are various interpretations for this. You can rule out potential causes by reading about all the diseases and pests in this chapter. Starvation, the bees freezing to death, an abundance of wetness, or chemical exposure are possible additional explanations.

Lack of activity: When there isn't much activity and it's not winter, it's time to open your hive and look inside.

- Outside the hive, there might be a lot more bee poop than normal.

Things you can see inside the hive that may be a sign that something isn't quite right include:

Missing queen: Also get in touch with your bee mentor and a nearby or online beekeeper who offers queens. Without the queen, a colony cannot thrive.

More than one egg per cell: If there are too many eggs in each cell, you have egg-laying workers. Because worker eggs are not fertilized, they will all develop into drones. Additionally, a colony doesn't require that many drones because they will consume all the resources without contributing to any effort.

Foul smell: The foul smell is not the same as the nasty stench emanating from a sickly brood. You may have AFB if you smell something bad.

Funny-looking brood: It refers to something that appears unusual.

- The hive is not being cleaned by the bees.
- The bees are generating numerous queen cells, supersedure cells, or queen cells out of regular brood cells.

The Most Common Pests and What to Do About Them

Beehives may become infested by pathogenic bacteria, fungi, viruses, mites, and pests. Despite of all the chaos that bees may encounter, a healthy hive can perform an amazing job of defending its colony. Cleaners in hives are always working to keep the hive and all the bees clean. For further security at their home's entrance, they keep guard bees.

But there will be occasions when you must intervene and assist them. If you find yourself having to treat your hive, be careful to alternate your treatments to prevent the bacteria and pests from developing a tolerance to whatever you are doing.

American Foulbrood (AFB) and European Foulbrood EFB)

The spore-forming bacteria that cause AFB and EFB are infectious and extremely contagious diseases. The larvae and pupae are affected, not the adult bees. The hive gets a bad stench from this sickness, hence the name.

The evidence is visible in the brood cells in addition to the smell. Infected larvae change color to a caramel-chocolate shade and dissolve into a gooey mess on the cell floor as opposed to normal pearly-white larvae. After the cell is sealed, they always perish. AFB is more serious than EFB (although still very dangerous). The larvae of an EFB infection are twisted inside the brood cell and start out as an off-white color before turning brown. They pass away before the cell is sealed.

Also Check For:

- A spotted pattern on the brood
- Off-center holes in the brood cell caps
- Sunken cappings on the brood cells

- Caramel color of dead larvae
- Scales on the larvae

You must get in touch with your neighborhood extension office or beekeepers association if you think you may have AFB or EFB. State legislation may govern how infected hives are handled and disposed of. Unfortunately, there is no salvaging your colony if it contracts AFB or EFB. Once you've been in touch with your county extension, they will either come to dispose of your hive for you or they will provide you instructions. Extreme precautions must be used because the spores can live permanently on beekeeping equipment and are highly contagious.

Varroa Mite

The parasitic Varroa mite feeds on honeybee blood and the blood of the young. Only a honeybee colony can reproduce it. The bees become less strong and live less time due to these vampire arachnids. The mature female mite has eight legs and a flattened oval-shaped body that is reddish brown in color. These annoyances should be visible to the unaided eye.

You can use a variety of chemical remedies to get rid of Varroa mites. They consist of oxalic acid, Apistan, CheckMite+, Apistan, Mite Away Quick Strips, Formic Pro, Apivar, Hopguard II, Apivar Life Var, and Apistan. There will be specific application instructions for each therapy.

Deformed Wing Virus

Although it can occur in colonies that haven't been infected with Varroa, this viral disease is linked to infestations with those mites. It could result in bees developing wings that are deformed, twisted, or wrinkled. These bees are obviously unable to fly and are unable to assist their colony. Controlling the Varroa mite population is the best strategy for combating the deformed-wing virus.

Sacbrood

A virus called sacbrood attacks a honeybee brood, primarily worker bee larvae. With inconsistent cappings present throughout the brood cells, the sacbrood virus generates an uneven brood pattern. Because it inhibits the brood from reaching the pupa stage, this disease is relatively simple to identify.

In most situations, a strong hive can defeat sacbrood disease on its own, while severe cases can necessitate replacing the queen.

Bee Louse

An infrequent pest of bees, the bee louse is a tiny, wingless member of the fly family. Although it is not a sickness of the bees, it does cause a lot of stress on colonies, which makes them weaker.

Although they only have six legs, bee-louse adults resemble Varroa mites somewhat. Adults should add a small amount of tobacco to their smoker and puff on the hive to treat their condition. Despite having a worm-like appearance, the larvae are very difficult to discern with the unaided eye. Than real larvae, comb damage is more likely to be observed. The frames should be wrapped in plastic and frozen for 48 hours to kill any bee-louse larvae present. By doing so, you'll guarantee that both adults and larvae are killed.

Tracheal Mite

This small spider is a respiratory system parasite that attacks honeybees. Drones, queen bees, and worker bees are all susceptible to infection. The bee is killed after it consumes blood and reproduces inside its breathing tubes. Indicators include an increase in winter fatalities and a decrease in spring brood production.

If you think you may have tracheal mites, your county extension office could arrange a test. The recommended course of action includes requeening the hive along with the use of menthol and fat patties consisting of vegetable shortening and sugar (which prevent mite reproduction).

Wax Moth

Beeswax combs, comb honey, and pollen harvested by bees are all harmed by the bug known as the wax moth. For weak colonies, they are primarily a problem. Even if you're the best beekeeper in the world, wax moths are a problem that all hives must deal with eventually.

Reduce the amount of empty space in your hive to help fend off a wax moth invasion. Add boxes only if your hive requires them. Wax moths will take control of the hive if no one is present to protect it. Wrapping the affected frame in a plastic bag and freezing it for 48 hours is another method of treating wax moth infestations. Additionally, you can fumigate your colony using crystals of paradichlorobenzene (PDB).

Small Hive Beetle

Nearly all honeybee hives are home to this invasive insect. Small hive beetles will proliferate if given the chance and seriously harm your colony. Nearly all beekeepers will have to deal with them, just like the wax moth.

Although there are various pharmaceutical remedies, little hive beetle avoidance is the greatest line of protection. Limit the amount of space that is available in the hive, just like with the wax moth. Apply a board with a wire bottom and a tray underneath it to the bottom of your Warre or Langstroth hive. On the tray, spread some dish soap. The insects will drop into the tray and become trapped there.

Chapter 3
Beeswax

Beeswax is a type of organic wax that is used by worker bees to create "combs" that will eventually hold their honey. Additionally, it is frequently used to recycle and repair preexisting combs.

The primary components of beeswax are fatty acids and natural alcohol. The wax is produced by a particular gland in the abdomen of worker bees, which essentially converts pollen's sugar into the wax by processing it; the pollen they gather contributes to the wax's "golden" hue.

In addition to being ideal for building the hive, beeswax is a terrific ingredient for cosmetic products like lip balm because it is so durable and stable (particularly in hot and cold weather conditions).

Fun fact: Bees must ingest five to six days' worth of pollen to generate beeswax.

Safety and Precautions

How to Harvest Beeswax

We'll go over the best way to accomplish it below if you want to extract beeswax yourself. The "Melt and Strain Method" is what is used in this process.

1. Collect the "Capping" and Comb

Remove the caps off your frames with a tool (just the wax that covers the combs). While you should make every effort to get all the honey out, some may inevitably come out. Don't stress about it too much; we'll strain the honey later.

After gathering the comb, place it in cheesecloth to drain the honey (place the fabric over a container to capture the honey to prevent a mess!).

2. Separate the Wax From the "Debris."

Place the cheesecloth-wrapped beeswax bundle inside a small bundle and into a pan of simmering water. If there are any large lumps, you can press them down with anything like a wooden spoon or stick to assist the wax to melt more quickly.

Boiling water should be used, and after the beeswax has completely melted, it should be squeezed to extract as much liquid as possible. The cheesecloth should then be removed from the pot, leaving "wax water" behind.

The solution should be poured into a container and left to cool. All the filthy water will eventually sink below the wax, which will eventually rise to the surface. We must clean the wax "cake" above because it will still be unclean.

3. Clean the Wax Cake

After the solid wax cake has completely cooled, remove it from the liquid and remelt it. When it becomes liquid again, any leftover bad stuff is removed by passing it through a filter while it is still hot.

4. Put into a Mold

You ought to now have some beautiful, clean wax. If necessary, use it as a liquid or pour it into any mold you have, and you're done!

Don't overlook one of the most valuable and plentiful components of your hive, beeswax, as there are so many fantastic uses for it.

Benefits of Beeswax

Beeswax is used as a common ingredient in a wide variety of products, from food to cosmetics, for many good reasons. Here are a few of the most intriguing ones:

- Because it is insoluble in water, it is incredibly practical as a sealant for wood protection or for use in crafts. This is also the rationale for our recommendation to combine it with linseed oil before using it to seal your wooden beehive.

- Making candles with beeswax is one of the best uses for the material because the wax burns cleanly and doesn't emit smoke or chemicals. According to some, burning beeswax releases negative ions that purify the air by removing "positive charge" airborne contaminants like dust.

- Beeswax has a relatively low melting point of 63 degrees Celsius (about 145 degrees Fahrenheit), which makes it quite simple to transform it from a solid to a liquid for use in a variety of applications.

- Beeswax is far from a straightforward substance; it contains more than 250 different elements such as acids, long-chain alkanes, esters, and others. Hentriacontane makes up around 9% of beeswax, which is why it is so stable and insoluble in water.

How Can I Use Beeswax?

You've come to the correct place if you have beeswax on hand and are unsure of what to do with it. There are many more applications for beeswax than those we have listed below.

Never throw away beeswax since it is so helpful and versatile.

- Cosmetics ingredients (lip balm etc.)
- Pharmaceutical uses
- Official documents seal

- Skincare ingredients (soap etc.)
- Woodcare
- Food production
- Crafts
- Waxing products
- Candles

Chapter 4
Modern Beekeeping

This beekeeper usually uses roach baits in high traps, chemical mite traps, feeds bees fructose corn syrup, and even makes hives die especially during the process of almond pollination.

The idea of a modern beekeeper is not to harm the bees but to help ensure their health for great returns. Here are the pros and cons of a modern commercial beekeeper to help you decide.

Pros

• Massive amounts of honey and pollen production, which means more income

• More experience in the short term

Cons

• Having to rebuild constantly due to colony losses

• The equipment is expensive

• The quality of the honey is low due to the chemicals

• Usually, a very non bee friendly approach

• Has many expenses

• Constantly dealing with hive pests and diseases.

The Treatment-free Beekeeper

Just like the title suggests, this kind of beekeeping usually dictates that you don't use any treatment. Instead, you can help better your bees and you depending on the beehive configuration you use.

If you decide to be this kind of beekeeper, you must avoid using Langstroth style beehives, especially interior plastic designs. This is because the comb, which is the foundation of the health of your beehive, is not cycled enough to maintain a homeostatic environment.

This means that this kind of beekeeper would do better using the Warre or Top Bar Style beehives. This is where there is constant harvesting of the comb.

Remember that the health of your colony is crucial. Therefore, the first step is allowing the bees to make new combs when necessary. When you use chemicals and pesticides, they get stored in older combs that create a foundation for poor health. Here are the pros and cons of being this kind of beekeeper.

Pros

• Reduced labor for the beekeeper.

• Less in-hive disturbance and interference.

- It reduces the personal time to care for the hive and fewer expenses on the supplies needed.

Cons

- Reduced amounts of honey.

- Generally, the bees are less productive.

- The hives are difficult to keep alive.

- Reduced success in maintaining the health of an apiary.

- Constantly must deal with pests and diseases.

The Chemical-free Beekeeper Who Treats

Unlike the previous form of beekeeping, this method requires the beekeeper to use non-harmful intervention, mainly because he/she is aware of the many challenges a modern bee faces, which is why they try to help them out.

Therefore, this means that instead of using harmful treatments, for example, in treating varroa mites, you choose a thermosolar or oxalic acid treatment. A beekeeper following this method requires extensive research to make sure they are aware of their many alternatives.

This type of beekeeping works best with a Top Bar and Langstroth style beehives. They are both best suited for this type because they allow for an easier hive inspection.

Pros

- It gives the bees a stronger ability to make a crop and forage

- It gives the bees a chance for the need to thrive as a colony.

- Allows for the beekeeper to be in constant supervision of the hive.

- It increases the chances of having a harvestable crop.

Cons

- If not done correctly, the bees can get harmed.

- The tools required can get pricey.

- Some methods are unusable with honey in the hive.

These are the three kinds of beekeepers you can be. So it is up to you to figure out what best works for you. The next thing for you to learn is the best beehive configurations at your disposal.

Honey Extraction

Before you can enjoy your own personal treat or sell your honey, you must first collect it from the hives. First, ensure that you have enough funds to support your bees and have access to a suitable honey extractor. While not necessary, using an extractor will make the process much cleaner and easier. If you do not have one, consider borrowing from a fellow beekeeper in your club. To set yourself up for success, place a bee escape in the gap between the brood and honey boxes. This device will only allow bees to travel in one direction, making it easier to collect honey later on. For those with less time, there are options like Bee-Quick which repels bees with its scent. Once all preparations have been made, begin the harvesting process by suiting up and smoking he hive as you would during an inspection. Remove frames that are at least three-quarters capped and take them away from the hive. Store them in a room temperature area to soften them up before enjoying their sweet contents.

Choose your harvesting location carefully—no matter what, it will get at least a little messy, so it is best to have that all sorted and set up before working with the honey. Honey extraction (when using an extractor) then happens in these steps:

1. **Remove wax caps off the comb**. This is easily done with a heated electric knife. Starting from the top, carefully cut away the wax, leaving as much honey and comb behind as possible.

a. These wax caps are your stored beeswax, which can be used and sold as well.

2. **Place the cleaned frames into the extractor, trying to balance out the weight of frames on either side**. Start the extractor spinning with a bucket to collect the honey underneath the spout.

a. Most extractors only remove honey from one side at a time, so you will need to flip the frames to make sure both sides are emptied.

b. How fast the honey flows depend on the machine and the temperature of the honey—the warmer it is, the faster it moves.

3. **Once all the honey is off the frames, return them to the hive**. The bees will then clean them the rest of the way.

4. **For the honey, leave it for a while in the buckets or jars so that all air rises to the top and escapes**. After that, it is good to be bottled and stored.

And that is it! It is a pretty simple process and only requires a few different steps from a normal inspection. If you can't get access to a honey extractor, you can also hang the frames in a warm space (not direct sun) and let the honey drip into some buckets, but that will take longer.

There are two other methods to harvest honey—comb honey and the crush-and-strain method. Comb honey is perhaps the simplest since instead of cutting the caps off, you just cut the comb up altogether and package it with the honey. This may not sound good, but apparently, it is very tasty and the desired bonus by some people. The crush-and-strain method is very similar to comb honey, though after cutting the comb into pieces, it is squeezed or strained to remove as much of the honey from the wax as possible. The leftover wax then gets discarded.

Honey Recipes

Skin and Beauty

◇◇

Brown Sugar Honey Scrub

This brown sugar honey scrub is better than anything you can buy at the store and, best of all, it is inexpensive to make! Use this scrub daily for the best results.

Ingredients:

- 2 tablespoons raw honey
- 2 tablespoons dark brown sugar

Instructions:

1. Combine the ingredients in a small bowl and stir well.
2. Wash your face then apply about ½ teaspoon of the mixture to damp skin.
3. Massage the scrub into your face in a circular motion for 1 minute.
4. Rinse well with warm water then pat dry.
5. Store the extra in an air-tight container at room temperature.

◇◇

Honey Lemon Facial Hair Remover

If you are tired of shaving or bleaching your facial hair, this natural remedy is both gentle and effective. Made with natural ingredients like honey and lemon, this facial hair remover is the only recipe you will ever need.

Ingredients:

- 1 tablespoon raw honey
- ½ tablespoon ground oats
- 3 to 5 drops fresh lemon juice

Instructions:

1. Stir together the ingredients in a small bowl to form a paste.
2. Spread the paste on your face like you would apply a mask.
3. Leave the paste on for 15 minutes then rinse with warm water.
4. Repeat 2 to 3 times per week for 3 to 4 weeks.

Honey-Cucumber Facial Toner

This honey-cucumber facial toner is a gentle and natural way to hydrate your skin. Use this toner daily to give your skin a heathy glow.

Ingredients:

- 1 medium seedless cucumber
- 2 teaspoons raw honey

Instructions:

1. Peel and chop the cucumber then puree it in a food processor.
2. Strain the cucumber through fine mesh or cheesecloth and collect the juice.
3. Stir the honey into the juice then transfer the mixture to a small bottle.
4. Apply the toner to clean skin using a cotton ball in the morning and in the evening.
5. Let the mixture air dry then rinse with warm water.
6. Store the bottle in the refrigerator for 1 week.

Natural Remedies

Honey Treatment for Sinus Problems

Whether you are plagued by sinus pressure, excessive sneezing, or a persistently runny nose, this honey treatment for sinus problems is just what you need. When taken consistently, this treatment can help to reduce the frequency of sinus problems.

Ingredients:

- 1 tablespoon raw honey

Instructions:

1. Take the honey by mouth at bedtime.
2. Repeat daily to reduce the occurrence of sinus problems.

Fever-Reducing Honey Tea

This fever-reducing tea is a gentle and all-natural way to relieve even the most stubborn of fevers. Add more honey to taste, if needed, and drink two to three times daily until your fever dissipates.

Ingredients:

- 8 ounces hot water
- 1 teaspoon holy basil
- 1 teaspoon raw honey
- ¼ teaspoon fresh ground pepper

Instructions:

1. Combine the basil and water and let it steep for 5 minutes.

2. Stir in the black pepper and honey.

3. Sip the tea two to three times daily until your fever is gone.

Honey Hiccup-Stopper

Having a case of the hiccups can turn from funny to painful if it lasts too long. If holding your breath doesn't work, try this easy honey hiccup-stopper. It may not taste good, but it is sure to work!

Ingredients:

- 1 teaspoon raw honey

- 1 teaspoon castor oil

Instructions:

1. Stir together the ingredients in a small bowl.

2. Dip your finger into the mixture and lick it off.

3. Repeat every 10 minutes until your hiccups stop.

Conclusion

re You Ready to Begin Beekeeping? The end is near. I have given you all the necessary information to start a successful beekeeping enterprise, passing on everything I have discovered throughout my years of experience. Your dedication to preserving these essential insects is truly admirable. It's astonishing to think about, but it's undeniable - we and bees rely on each other for our existence. Whether one wishes to raise bees as a hobby or as a business, anyone can make a difference. Upon learning that you keep bees, you will quickly discover that everyone you meet will be delighted. Prior to the installation of your hive, there will be an influx of honey requests.

Remember that you can learn from other people. Consult your local beekeepers for assistance and refer to this manual for troubleshooting and assistance with any problems you may encounter. Practical experience is the only thing I cannot offer you. But you'll make it.

Book 5

Build your Beekeeping Equipment

Introduction

Place the collected material in a place where the hives blow dry, in the wind, and good sunlight.

When trying to decide where to find your apiary, consider the following:

Sources of nectar and pollen: While honey bees travel up to 3 miles or more in search of food, they prefer easy access, 300-500 meters from the hive. The feed should be available in one form or another during the season - from early spring to autumn.

Bees need water: Like all other living things on the planet, bees need water to survive. Not only do they drink water, but they also use it to restore crystallized honey and make bee bread - a mixture of honey and pollen that feeds the developing larva. If there is no natural water source nearby, such as a lake or stream, consider placing a birdbath or 2-gallon dog water bath near the hives.

Exposure to sunlight: Ideally, the hives should face south, fairly south. However, partial shading or spotted sunlight can have a beneficial effect on the hive during high sunlight and summer heat.

Wind protection: Nestle hives against shrubs or forest edges; place them next to a shed, garage, or other outbuildings to protect the colonies from the prevailing strong winds - this is especially important if you live in a climate where winter can let cool winds down over the hives.

Keep the hives dry: Bees are prone to many fungal diseases that are promoted in wet conditions, so choose a place for the hive to stay dry and provide good drainage during spring vinegar and long rains. Also, consider tilting the hives a little forward so that the moisture that accumulates inside the hives condenses off the hives instead of dripping onto the bees and egg nests.

Chapter 1
DIY Apiary

Types of Beehives

There are many different beehive types to choose from, and the type each beekeeper opts for might vary depending on their location, local climate, or preferred maintenance style.

The three popular choices are **the Langstroth, the Top-Bar, and the Warre,** so we'll discuss each one here, alongside some of their advantages.

As with many things, there is no perfect solution; each hive design has pros and cons. Carefully consider these before choosing the best one for you. The most important point to remember is that there is **no right or wrong way.**

Firstly, let's look at the Langstroth hive.

The Warre Hive

The Warre hive is pretty like to the Langstroth in terms of its shape and design. This one was created by a French monk called Abbé Émile Warré, whose vision for this hive **mirrors the bee's natural environment.** Due to this, the inside of a Warre hive is similar to a hollow tree, where many wild bees choose to build their hive.

The key difference between a Langstroth and Warre hive is that **when adding new boxes to a Warre hive, you add them below the existing boxes.** With the Langstroth, they go on top. Also, the Warre boxes are also typically a little smaller and lighter.

Another difference is **the Warre hive often doesn't use foundations**, so bees naturally create comb branching vertically.

The Warre hive's roof (quilt box) is also good at absorbing condensation, which bees really hate.

Overall, it **requires less maintenance**, which might appeal to new beekeepers.

The Langstroth Hive

The Langstroth hive is the **typical beehive image** that most people think of when you mention beekeeping- the box that has stacked layers. This beehive was created by Rev. LL Langstroth in 1852.

The general idea behind Langstroth is that it's **easy to use, easy to expand, and easy to access**. The breakthrough innovation of this hive design was the inclusion of frames that are **vertically hanging.**

This design also ensured that the gaps between the frames would be at least ¼", thus **accommodating sufficiently for bee space.**

Expanding a Langstroth hive is as simple as adding another layer.

Another huge advantage of the Langstroth hive is that the dimensions of this hive are **universally standard-** so if you buy parts of the hive from various vendors, you shouldn't have too many issues with inconsistent sizing.

The Top-Bar Hive

The design of the top bar is completely different from the others. Instead of a stacked, layered design, it's a simple "bathtub"-like shape with frames that run along it.

We'll cover the top bar in much more detail later in this book, so we'll keep it simple for now.

The advantages of the top-bar hive are that **the frames are much easier to access, and the overall structure is simpler.** You'll see in the next section how many different parts a typical hive requires- but the top-bar hive doesn't need a lot of them. **It's easy to use, highly simplistic**, and, similarly to the Warre hive, mirrors bees' natural environment as it lacks foundations.

The Hive Set-Up

The levels of a typical beehive are as follows (the point at the top of the list reflects the real top of the beehive, with the list proceeding downwards as a beehive would):

Top of the hive

*   Outer Cover
*   Feeders (internal hive top feeders)
*   Inner Cover
*   Honey Super/Extracting Super
*   Queen Excluder
*   Frames
*   Brood Box
*   Slatted Rack
*   Entrance Reducer
*   Bottom Board
*   Hive Stand

Ground

Let's examine the beehive structure in further depth and dissect each layer individually. This design is based on the popular Langstroth hive, but many hives (including the Top-Bar hive we'll teach you how to build later) have a similar structure.

Outer Cover

The outer cover, also referred to as a "telescoping cover," serves as the hive's ceiling. It is necessary to shield your hive and its inhabitants from adverse weather conditions. Generally, outside covers are flat and topped with a metal sheet (such as aluminum, zinc, steel, or copper) to provide greater protection against rain. The material of the outer cover is vital, but it is more necessary to ensure that the dimensions of the cover are larger than the real hive to protect the entire hive. The outer cover should also fit snugly over the inner cover's edge for added protection.

Feeders

As previously stated, feeders are crucial because they provide food for your worker bees when there is little honey to go around. Even as intelligent and efficient as bees are, they occasionally require assistance. There are numerous varieties of feeders, some of which are attached to the entrance of the hive, some of which are placed between the frames inside the hive, and others of which are left outside haphazardly. The type selected is a matter of personal preference.

A significant advantage of internally located feeders is that they are less attractive to robber bees and other predators.

Additionally, it is far more convenient for your bees to have a food supply within their hive.

If you are placing your feeder internally, it must be right over the brood box so that the bees may easily access it. Don't forget to remove the queen excluder layer, since this will make it more difficult for the bees to reach the queen!

An internal hive top feeder is a common form of feeder. These are advantageous since they can carry a large quantity of sugar syrup and include unique accessories that prevent bees from drowning in the sugar syrup. This sort of feeder is optimal for feeding a big colony of bees from a single source.

A second alternative for a feeder is identical to the last one, but external: an external hive top feeder. Typically, these feeders consist of mason jars or plastic buckets filled with sugar syrup. These jars are normally inverted over the entry hole of the inner cover and encircled by an empty hive box. This approach is effective for preserving the syrup against robber bees and particularly adverse weather situations.

A feeding shim is one additional example of a regularly used feeder. A feeding shim is a second empty wooden box with the same size as a hive that contains feeding vessels. During the colder months, these are a popular option for feeding sugar candy to bees. As previously said, feeders are crucial because they provide food for your worker bees when there is little honey to go around. Even as intelligent and efficient as bees are, they occasionally require assistance. There are numerous varieties of feeders, some of which are attached to the entrance of the hive, some of which are placed between the frames inside the hive, and others of which are left outside haphazardly. The type selected is a matter of personal preference.

Inner Cover

The inner cover serves as the roof of the hive. It has a central entrance hole and an additional entrance notch on the front of the cover. This entry must face forward during installation of the cover. The apertures are crucial, as they ensure that the hive has adequate ventilation. These holes can also be used to inject feeders into the hive or to provide an escape route for bees during honey harvesting.

Plywood is the finest material for the inside cover, as other materials would droop over time, which is undesirable when trying to conserve space within the hive.

It's very easy for folks to attach their inside coverings improperly, so be careful when doing so! Inner coverings have a "summer" and "winter" position; for the majority of the year, you should keep them in the "summer" position. One side of the cover is flat, while the other features a frame with a small open gap around the edge. In order to place the cover for summer, the flat side should face down, while the framed side should face up. This arrangement allows an air gap between the inner and outer covers, which helps to cool the hive.

Honey Supers

The honey super resides above the queen excluder and brood boxes. This layer is responsible for storing the honey that your bees will diligently make. Super boxes are commonly available in two sizes, medium and shallow, and are typically smaller than the actual nest box. If you choose a smaller honey super, your bees will likely fill it with honey more evenly, although medium-sized honey supers are the most prevalent.

When harvesting honey from your hives, you will collect it from the supers. Just remember to leave sufficient honey for your bees to survive the winter.

Queen Excluder

The queen excluder is a layer that serves to divide the hive into two extremely crucial sections: the honey-storing section and the egg-laying section. Neither should be combined for obvious reasons. The queen excluder rests atop the brood box and consists of a type of mesh that the queen cannot pass through (hence the name). It restricts the queen's access to the honey supers, preventing her from laying eggs there.

There are queen excluders built from a variety of materials, including metal, plastic, and wood, among others.

The use of queen excluders is a bit controversial among beekeepers. Some see this layer as **an essential protocol for ensuring an organized and efficient hive, but others see it as unnecessary as it apparently causes stress for the worker bees** (who don't like squeezing through small holes and don't like to move anywhere without the queen). However, **if you're a beginner, we'd strongly recommend using one** as the techniques you'll need to use to avoid needing a queen excluder are a little more trickier.

Frames

Every single type of beehive uses some type of frame. **A beehive without frames is simply not a beehive.** A beehive's frame shape will depend on the type of hive, but it'll always be there in some form.

The frame is the base on which the bees will construct their honeycomb. For beekeepers, the act of making honeycomb is referred to as "drawing comb."

Frames often have a " foundation " sheet on them; basically, a *hexagonal pattern made out of pressed wax or plastic.* This pattern **acts as a template the bees can use to build their honeycomb onto-** it helps the comb come out neater and more concise. But of course, a foundation sheet is not an essential thing to use; **some beekeepers prefer not to use them at all.** Frames without foundation are appropriately named "foundationless frames."

The frames themselves are **typically made from wood,** but it's not unheard of for beekeepers to use plastic. Of course, the size of the frame you use needs to match the size of your hive. Frames will come available in three sizes: **shallow, medium, and deep**. The "deep" frames are usually found in brood boxes, as they need to be a little bigger. Whereas shallow and medium frames are most used for honey supers of a corresponding size.

Most frames you can buy on the market come in similar sizes, but every brand won't be perfectly the same- so make sure to check the frames can fit into the hive you have/prior to purchasing them.

To avoid problems with compromised bee space (see the following section for additional information on bee space), it is advisable to use frames of the same type and size within the same hive.

Brood Box

The brood box is the lowest box in the hive, and it is where the queen lays her eggs. It is also the residence of the queen. The brood box must be the largest component of the hive in order to facilitate the colony's expansion over the proper season. If the brood box lacks adequate space, a second brood box can be installed to provide additional space.

A brood box is composed of many frames that bees utilize to construct wax comb. The number of frames in the brood box varies on the type of hive (but it will probably be around 8 or 10). If you don't mind the extra weight, 10 frames is OK, but if you need to transfer your hive, keep this in mind, since a 10-frame brood box can become quite heavy very soon. For a lighter hive, fewer frames are preferable. If your goal is to produce as much honey as possible and grow your colony, a 10-frame box may be more suitable.

Additional: brood boxes are also known as "brood chambers," "deep hive bodies," and "deep supers" or "brood supers." However, the inclusion of "super" in the name may confuse novice beekeepers; ensure that the brood box and honey supers are not mistaken for one another, as they are two distinct and vital components. Separating the super honey layer and the brood boxes should be a queen excluder. Don't get them confused!

Slatted Rack (Optional)

This is an optional portion of the hive, as the name indicates, but many beekeepers swear by them, so it depends on your preference. A slatted rack, also known as a brood rack, is a component of a hive that prevents problems including congestion and ventilation. During the height of the season, when your hive is at its densest, it can become somewhat congested. Using a slatted rack gives the bees a bit more room to roam around beneath the brood box. It's useful for minimizing overpopulation and maintaining ventilation in your hive.

Adding more space with a slatted rack helps keep your hive warmer in the winter.

If you choose to utilize a slatted rack, you must ensure that it is installed correctly. A slatted rack will have a deep and shallow side; the shallow side should face up and be aligned with the frames of your brood box. If you do not place it in this manner, the bees will likely cover the extra space with burr comb, making it more difficult to manage and remove the frames from the brood box.

Entrance Reducer

The role of the entrance reducer is **literally to reduce the size of the entrance to the hive.** This part is located snugly between the bottom board and the lowest hive box, and they're very useful for controlling movement into the hive. They can also be used to prevent other pests from entering your hive (e.g., stopping field mice from entering the hive in the winter months). If your hive gets "robbed" by predators, **having a limited entrance space helps bees be able to defend the hive more easily.**

The entrance reducer is a long piece of wood with several different-sized holes acting as entrances. The wood is adjusted by turning it to change the entrance size to the hive.

The main piece of advice we can give when shopping for this piece of gear is to buy an entrance reducer from the same manufacturer that makes your other hive parts. This is to avoid frustration, as different brands are not the most consistent when it comes to sizing.

Bottom Board

The bottom board is essentially the floor of the hive. There are two types: solid or screened.

Screened: a screened bottom board is **great for ventilation** as it is a mesh screen typically made from wire or plastic. It helps to r**egulate an appropriate temperature within the hive** and can also **help limit humidity.** This screen board is also thought to be better at protecting the hive from pests such as moths or varroa (a type of mite that can cause a lot of problems in beehives). As the screen has holes in it, it allows things to fall through it, which **can also help to keep the hive a little cleaner.**

A decent-quality screened bottom board will come with some kind of tray that can be slid shut to close the bottom of the hive. This is useful during the colder months and when you want to inspect the hive.

Solid: as you might guess, a solid bottom board is a **board that has no holes**. Using this type, ventilation can be reduced greatly, and in colder weather, it has the advantage of keeping the bottom of the hive much warmer. The warmer hive will encourage bees to start getting to work (or brood rearing) earlier in the day. As solid bottom boards don't have holes for waste and other things to fall through, this type of board will catch a lot of various debris. Due to this, a solid bottom board needs to be cleaned regularly.

Hive Stand

The hive stand is the structure where the whole hive will be put on top, and it's a crucial part of the hive set-up for countless reasons. Firstly, it stops unwanted moisture from entering the hive. When it comes to wild beehives, they're typically located in trees or as high up as possible- because bees hate moisture and want to avoid humidity as much as possible. In fact, **if too much damp enters a hive, it can kill a bee colony.**

Another key reason to use a hive stand is that it'll be easier for you to maintain your hive. Having to bend over to do all necessary bee-related tasks can mess with your back, so having an elevated hive base will make life far easier.

The **perfect height for a hive stand is typically considered to be 2 feet/60 cm.**

When looking at what type of hive stand to buy, there are two types available: single and multiple. Single hive stands are often bought commercially, whereas beekeepers themselves often build multiple hive stands. The main benefit of having a multiple hive stand is **that there will be sufficient room between hives for inspecting them,** as inspection requires you to take apart your hive, and you'll need room to put these parts down. These hives stand types can *be made from wooden beams or cement blocks.*

If you're looking to build a multiple hive stand, just remember that the stand needs to support a lot of weight and be as level to the ground as possible.

You can also build single hive stands, but it's far easier to just buy one that you can simply assemble. Even if you're dealing with an uneven surface, a single hive stand can be stabilized easily; they're far more forgiving. Just make sure you're getting a hive stand that fits your hive size (depending on whether it's an 8 or 10-frame hive).

Depending on the type of hive stand you purchase, some will come with an additional landing board, which is a kind of ramp that bees going in and out of the hive can utilize. Most agree that a landing board is good additional equipment for new beekeepers, as **it gives them a chance to observe the colony before they disappear inside the hive.** Even a f*ew minutes of simple observation is enough to learn a lot about bees' habits and behaviors!*

But landing boards are not necessary for the bee's daily life, so **they are not essential pieces of kit to have.** In fact, experts say that these boards can hinder honeybees from living in certain climates. Also, in certain weather conditions, these ramps can pose a bit of a problem: if it snows, the entrance can get blocked, or if it rains, the bees can get stuck to it.

Chapter 2
Inspect the Apiary

One of the more enjoyable aspects of beekeeping is the thrill of inspecting the hive, which offers a chance to watch your bees go about their many activities. When we were new beekeepers, we had no idea what we were doing or what we should be looking for. Your hive inspection should be a time to enjoy your bees up close and personal while also observing their overall health. Be sure to gather up everything you will need before you open your hive. Always use a smoker to calm your bees. You will be looking at very tiny eggs, so choose the proper visual assistance to help you see clearly. We use reading glasses to help us see up close. You may be nervous your first time, unsure of what to expect, so wear the proper amount of protective gear to help build your confidence. Stay calm and enjoy the experience. How many people have the privilege of watching honeybees work up close? Work your inspection from the back or side. If you perform your inspection from the front, you will hinder the flight of foragers coming and going.

Timing

Develop a regular routine when it comes to inspecting your hive every two weeks. You do not have to perform a meticulous and thorough inspection that takes hours. Rather, you're specifically observing the productivity of your queen. You must verify that you see an abundance of eggs. When you see eggs, you know the queen was there to lay those eggs within the last day or two. Performing an inspection every two weeks confirms that your queen is healthy and has a great brood pattern. If you lose your queen and the colony fails to raise a new one, then after three weeks the hive begins spiraling into a tailspin, and it becomes more difficult to save. Inspecting every two weeks allows you to catch any queen issues in time to place a new queen in the hive before the hive begins to fail. Your main goal is to verify eggs and capped-over pupae in the colony.

When To Inspect

After you install your package, you will be excited to inspect the hive to see if the queen has been released from her cage. It is important to wait at least three days to allow the queen to exit her cage and become acquainted with the colony. If she is not released from the cage, you can either place the cage back in the hive or open the cage and allow her to walk out onto the frames. The queen's pheromone is an important factor in helping solidify the colony as a single superorganism. Be patient. The bees need time to eat through the candy in the queen cage to release her and to start building some comb on the new foundation.

When Not To Check

Our busy lives may interfere with the timing of inspecting our hive. For example, we may only have time in the morning before we leave for work or when we get home after work. This may not work. Inspecting bees too early in the day or too late in the day is not the best time. Bees are not foraging at these times, resulting in more bees being home in their hive. Avoid opening a hive for inspection when it is dark, raining, or during high winds. Never inspect your hive unless the temperature is above 60 degrees Fahrenheit.

How Often To Check

Looking in on your bees is one of the most fun and enjoyable aspects of beekeeping. Many new beekeepers worry that they are not inspecting enough or that they may be inspecting too often. What is the best approach in planning your hive inspections? Every two weeks is the happy medium. With a colony, we must be able to detect any issues early. Inspecting our hives every two weeks will give us the opportunity to address a problem before it gets out of hand. Frequent inspections will allow us to monitor how well our queen is laying eggs. Since the queen lays over 1,000 eggs a day, inspections that are too far apart could cause the colony to be very low in population from a failing queen. Inspecting every two weeks gives us an edge on making corrections by replacing the queen should she start to fail. It also allows us to know how well the foundation is being drawn out with wax or if we need to create more space by adding boxes to the hive. An inspection every two weeks also helps us keep an eye on any pests or diseases before they spread out of control.

Checking Too Much

Can you inspect the hive too often? Maybe, especially if your bees are extremely agitated by frequent inspections. Certainly, you can learn the art of inspecting a colony by keeping the bees as calm as possible. Until you develop this skill, limit your inspections to every two weeks, because a new beekeeper may squish and kill bees with clumsy handling of the frames. You do not want to accidentally kill your queen. Each inspection does break the propolis seal of the top cover. However, on warm days, it is quickly resealed by the weight of the top cover. It will not reseal on cooler days.

Observing

Much can be observed when walking up to the hive, even before opening the top. Look for anything unusual around the hive, such as an excessive number of dead bees in front of the hive. A small amount is normal. Also look for any unusual signs of animal tracks, such as those from skunks. Skunks will leave scratch marks on the ground and on the front of the hive. Look for bugs, such as yellow jackets, spiders, or moths. Listen to the sound of the bees. Can you hear a normal low hum? Are the bees moving normally in and out of the front entrance? Good, that's normal. If they are being robbed by another hive, there will be bees all around the hive. Are there any foul odors around the hive?

Chapter 3
Most Used Equipment

Beekeeping Tools

Considering beekeeping, then there are certain tools and equipment you'll need to do it successfully. Here is some of the equipment

Bee Hives: this is the home of the bees. There are different types of beehives, and selecting which to use is dependent on you and what you want to do with it. Some of the types are;

Langstroth Hive

This is the commonly used beehive, and it's best for any newbie. The name was derived from Rev. Lorenzo Langstroth, who patterned it in the 19th century. This hive is built up by boxes stacked on each other. There are seven boxes which are;

- Outer cover
- Inner cover
- Honey supers
- Queen excluder
- Deep super
- Bottom board
- Stand.

Horizontal Top Bar Hive

This is the oldest beehive. It consists of a long box with wooden bars laid on top of it. It does not require a foundation, and it is carried about. It does not need to be assembled, though it is good you add a stand to lift it from the ground. Extracting honey from this type of hive is not easy because you'll always need the comb and honey. You should check it often to avoid it from being overcrowded.

Emile Warre Hive

In the 20th century, Emile Warre a French beekeeper designed another top bar hive but not horizontal. Emile's vertical top bar hive with no frames or foundation though consists of stacked boxes.

Frames

These are rectangular-like objects hanging in the beehives where the bees build their comb, live their lives, lay brood, and make honey. One of the essential benefits of this frame is that it can be removed to inspect the bees to know if they have diseases or if you want to extract honey from the bees. Wooden frames are the old and traditional frame or bees, while plastic frames are an innovation.

There are some factors that one ought to consider when getting a frame. The frame should be very easy to work with. Otherwise, your bees would build honeycombs in the wrong places. Next, your beehive frame should be able to last for long. If you use an inferior material to build your frame, it could crack with time or during cleaning, which would cost a lot to repair.

The frame should also be easy to clean because you may need to scrape propolis out of it at intervals, or you may need to hose it or boil it. The frame should also be light yet sturdy for easy lifting.

Wooden Frames

Wooden frames have their advantages. Wood is a natural material and is bee friendly. This advantage makes it easy for them to adjust. They are also easy to repair when they are damaged. When they break, you can use their pieces to make other beehive frames. You can use wooden frames with both plastic and wax foundations. It is also easy to find wood for beehives.

Wooden hive frames also have their disadvantages. If you do not choose a strong wood, it could break when you are making the frame, and this would be a waste of your money and time. On the other hand, if you use a dense frame, it will make the beehive very heavy. Also, it would be difficult to pass nails and put staples when making the frame.

Plastic Frames

Plastic frames also have advantages and disadvantages. The various colors that the plastic frames come in are very handy when managing your bees. The white frames are perfect for honey, and the black frames could be used as brood chambers as it would be easy to identify eggs on them. Plastic frames are also more durable than wooden ones. They are pre-coated with wax, making it easy for the bees to adapt to them easily. Plastic frames also help to reduce invasion by pests and parasites as the insects and larvae will not pass through the frames, which will keep them from spreading. Another advantage is that the plastic frames are already assembled in the box and ready to use.

On the other hand, plastic is not organic and so cannot be used for organic beekeeping. Also, once

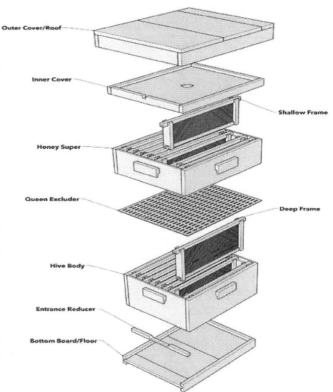

Outer Cover/Roof

Inner Cover

Shallow Frame

Honey Super

Queen Excluder

Deep Frame

Hive Body

Entrance Reducer

Bottom Board/Floor

the plastic frames are broken, you cannot use them again.

As already stated, there are different types of frames aside from the regular ones, and they include:

- Drone trap frames: there are specially crafted frames that some beekeepers design to encourage bees to build drone broods so that they can cut them out.

- Queen rearing frames: there are special frames like the cell bar frames used to grow new queens. Queen cups are placed vertically beside the bars so that the bees can build queen cells. When these cells are then capped, the beekeeper moves the cup to a colony with no queen for adoption.

Smoker

This is used for spreading smoke around the hive. Bees don't like smoke, so spreading smoke around their hive would keep them far and help you not to be stung. I will explain this properly later.

Hive Tool

This is for separating supers and frames; it is also for separating hive bodies. It is a multipurpose tool held with the hand and can be used to maintain and inspect beehives. They have multiple styles and variants.

It is the third most important tool that a beekeeper needs after the beekeeping veil and the bee smoker. There are two major kinds of hive tools: the standard hive tool and the J-type hive tool.

The standard hive tool comes with a box levering edge and a frame levering edge, while the J-type hive tool comes with a box levering edge, but instead of a frame levering edge, it comes with a j-hook and a small notch. Any of these hive tools could have a small hole that you could use to remove small nails. It works like a claw hammer.

The hive stool is also used when lifting frames when the hive has been protolyzed. There is a particular way to use the J-type. The J is inserted into the bee space, making the notch rest on the wall or frame behind to aid in the lifting. Please do not use the j-hook under the lugs of the frame because it will not fit and can cause breakages to the lugs of the frame.

Some people try to use a chisel or ordinary screwdriver instead of the hive tool. This is wrong as it could cause damage to the beehive or even to the equipment. As a result, it is not advisable to use these tools to inspect the hive.

The uses of a beehive are outline properly below:

- To pry things apart
- To scrape things off

The beekeeper can also use it for

- removing any propolis-glued bee cover that has been firmly adhered.
- To pry open boxes that propolis has caused to become glued together
- removing frames from the hive body when the situation warrants it.

- Taking off the brace, bridge, and burr combs.

- cleaning different parts of the hive's body of dirt and propolis.

- removing the cover from a bee package.

- removing a bee stinger without pressing on the venom sac and allowing more poison to enter the body.

Queen Catcher

When going through your hives, it is easy to lose the queen bee, so a queen catcher is used for separating the queen for a while.

Bee Suit

A bee suit would help prevent being stung by bees.

Gloves

With gloves, digging through a beehive would be safer. They should cover your arm well and of good material to save you from the pain of a sting. Gloves also protect the beekeeper from sticky things that come off easily like honey, sticky things that are tough to leave like propolis, and stings from bees. It is not enough to have thin gloves; you need thick impenetrable leather that protects the elbow.

Boots

These are not just fancy boots, but protective boots that go up to the knees. The material should be strong enough and the sole too to prevent being stung through them.

Oils: This is essential and can be used for a lot of things. You can use it to drive out beetles that want to dominate the hive. It is also used for attracting bees and as a supplement for the bees.

Feeders

This is where the food you mixed yourself is placed for the bees to feed on. This is better used instead of open feeding where other creatures can partake of this food, reducing it for the bees.

Sugar: buying sugar in a large quantity is expedient as there are times when the bees would need you to help supplement their food supply which syrup is made from a mixture of equal amounts of sugar and water.

Queen Excluder

This is like a grater that is used to stop or restrict the queen from going to a particular area. The holes are wide enough to let the worker bees and other bees pass through but too small for the queen.

The excluders could be a disadvantage because most times, worker bees are not used to passing through an excluder and so are intimidated and then stay back in the lower brood box. This could lead to a less efficient hive. It could also lead to quick filling of the brood box, and then there will be hive swarming due to overcrowding.

Queen Marker

Finding the queen bee can be very difficult and frustrating, so marking the queen early is important. This tool is used to mark the queen and save you the stress of finding it later.

Chapter 4
Building Hives

Most of the beehives we have discussed are not easy to get, and some might not meet your needs. Therefore, the best thing to do is build a beehive that meets your exact needs and is perfectly efficient.

Building a beehive might seem difficult, but it is easier than you think. All you need are the right tools and the right guidance to create a great standard beehive.

The design we're going to build is a Langstroth hive, the most used, and that you can customize based on the size of your colony. You can always keep adding and building depending on how many bees you have.

The idea is to revert to the industrialized way of obtaining honey that involves 10,000 and 30,000 bees.

Tools required

- Drill
- Dado stack
- Tin snips
- Miter saw
- Table saw

Materials required

- 1 by 10 board
- 1 by 2 board
- 1-½" trim head screws
- ¼" plywood
- 2" trim head screws
- 1 by 3 board

cutting list

Key	Qty	Material	Dimensions	Part
Bottom Board/Floor				
A	2	1x3 board	3/4" x 2-1/2" x 22"	Sides
B	1	1x3 board	3/4" x 2-1/2" x 2"	Back
C	2	1x10 board	3/4" x 9-1/4" x 15-1/4"	Floor board
D	1	1x10 board	3/4" x 2-3/4"* x 15-1/4"	Floor board
Entrance Reducer				
E	1	1x3 board	3/4" x 7/8" x 14-1/2"	Entrance reducer
Hive Body				
F	2	1x10 board	3/4" x 9-1/4" x 14-1/2"	Ends
G	2	1x10 board	3/4" x 9-1/4" x 19-3/4"	Sides
H	4	1x3 board	3/4" x 2-1/2" x 5"	Handles
Honey Super				
J	2	1x10 board	3/4" x 6" x 14-1/2"	Ends
K	2	1x10 board	3/4" x 6" x 19-3/4"	Sides
L	4	1x3 board	3/4" x 2-1/2" x 5"	Handles
Frame (Qty based on one frame)				
M	1	1x2 board	3/4" x 3/4" x 19"	Top bar
N	2	1x2 board	3/4" x 1-1/4" x 8-1/2"	End bars
P	1	1x2 board	3/4" x 3/4" x 17"	Bottom bar
Inner Cover				
Q	2	1x2 board	3/4" x 1-1/2" x 19-3/4"	Sides
R	2	1x2 board	3/4" x 1-1/2" x 14-1/2"	Ends
S	1	1/4" plywood	1/4" x 14-1/2" x 19"	Center board
Outer Cover/Roof				
T	2	1x3 board	3/4" x 2-1/2" x 21-7/8"	Sides
U	2	1x3 board	3/4" x 2-1/2" x 16-1/4"	Ends
V	2	1x10 board	3/4" x 9-1/4" x 17-3/4"	Top board
W	1	1x10 board	3/4" x 3"* x 17-3/4"	Top board
X	1	Aluminum	Cut to fit	Aluminum top

*Scribe and cut to fit

The Project Plans

Procedure

1.   Start by cutting A-D using the miter saw, then center a ¾" by ⅜" deep dado into side A. Next, fasten side B with glue and 2" trim head screws.

2.   Place the two one by ten floorboards into place, then place the final floorboard into place before ripping the board into the scribbled width of the table saw. Next, glue and screw the floorboards into

the right place.

3.   Now crosscut the 1" by 3" to 14 ½", rip it to ⅞" using the table saw, then set up your dado stack to cut ¾" by ⅜" deep notch.

4.   Next, cut a 3" wide notch at the entrance reducer, 3" from one end. Next, rotate the entrance by 90°, then make one pass 4" from the other end.

5.   Crosscut the parts again to length before cutting a 3/8" by ¾" into the edge of a wide rabbet using a sacrificial fence. Fasten the sides of the body hive using glue and screws.

6.   Now cut a ⅜" by a ¾" wide rabbet into a 22" using a table saw before crosscutting the four 5" long handles out of the 1 by 3.

7.   Try and center the handles on each body on each face about 1¼" from the rabbeted edge, then fasten it in place using glue and screws.

8.   To create the frames, cut a ½" into two ¾" then crosscut them to 19" before ripping and crosscutting a 1 by 2 into a 1 1/4" by 8 ½." Cut a ¾" by ¾" notch into the center of each board.

9.   Now cut a ¼" by ⅜" groove into the center of each part to create the top bar. Next, slowly place the beeswax foundation under the frame of the bottom bar before drilling pilot holes from the end bars and into the top or bottom bars.

10.   The next thing is to crosscut the 1 by 2 to length before cutting a ¼" by ⅜" dado into the center of the 14 ½" ends. Now cut a ¾" by ⅜" deep notch on the center of one of the 14 ½". Crosscut and rip the ¼" plywood to the required size for the centerboard.

11.   Take the aluminum and cut with tin snips to 2" longer and wider than the box before placing the wood at the center of the outline of the assembly and center of the aluminum. Glue the aluminum to the surface using construction adhesive until it sticks properly.

12.   For a smooth corner, hammer the edges of the aluminum using a mallet.

That is just about everything you need to know about beehives and how to construct the perfect one for you that suits your needs. The next thing to learn is getting the right bees for you.

conclusion

Only the most dedicated and successful beekeepers possess a fierce passion for their craft. They live and breathe honeybees, constantly seeking to expand their knowledge and understanding of these tiny creatures. Understanding how bees thrive without human intervention is paramount in truly comprehending their behavior and complex biochemistry.

Final Words

For others, beekeeping is among the most pleasurable activities available. Apart from the pleasure of caring for the bees, beekeeping provides a delicious reward - honey!

However, there are additional benefits, the most significant of which is that bees assist in pollinating the plants in the community gardens and crop fields. Pollination is an important, if not the most important, factor in increasing the output of vegetables, fruits, and harvests.

You've probably heard the saying "as busy as a bee" before. Indeed, bees are naturally quite active. They work extremely diligently to bring nectar into the hive. Bees have a life expectancy of nearly 35 days. After that, their wings become worn down to the point where they are no longer useful to their community. That is when they will perish.

Bees store honey for times of famine - when there are no flowers in the area. There are seasons when flowers are abundant for bees to harvest nectar. The ecstatic bees generate far more than they can consume. Beekeepers have a bumper crop of honey this time of year. Selling honey is another way to get money.

Honey is classified into two categories. To begin, beekeepers sell honey collected from hives. It is honey in liquid form. Beekeepers who use centrifuge equipment can remove the honeycombs. These are colloquially referred to as extractors. However, beekeepers can sell honeycomb by splitting it into pieces!

Many people prefer to purchase honey directly from the source in its original wax combs. Although the honey sold in this manner is not ready for use, it is a bonus for those who prefer natural products.

Most people are unaware that honey comes in various colors and flavors. Not all flowers have the same fragrance. Similarly, nectar from many varieties of flowers has a distinct aroma and flavor. Another factor affecting the taste/odor of honey is the soil.

Variation in soil type might also affect the appearance of your honey. For example, honey made from alfalfa nectar blooms on flowers cultivated in dry or alkaline soil. As a result, the honey you receive may range in color from white to clear.

On the other hand, honey made from buckwheat nectar typically thrives in acidic soils. As a result, they are quite dark. Also, the quality of the honeycomb can affect the color, appearance, and taste of the honey. Occasionally, honey is golden in hue, but it can also be red or green.

Generally, various state regulations govern the processing and manufacture of various honeybee products. A beekeeper needs to adhere to the state's regulations. Also, it's a good idea to determine whether any federal requirements regarding honey processing, labeling, and handling apply.

Remember that many people benefit from beekeeping, and it is a recognized business type under state legislation. In some circumstances, state governments have different regulations regarding beekeeping in a particular location.

Also, beekeepers should explore some unique marketing methods. This can assist them in selling honey and other bee products. Where to sell the honey and who the intended clients are are two important considerations for beekeepers to address

Nowadays, many hobbies are available, but beekeeping is perhaps the most rewarding. Therefore, refrain from attempting to hold on. Take aggressive measures to grow your beekeeping business!

Made in the USA
Columbia, SC
25 September 2024

43073025R00074